IBSEN

in an hour

BY RICK DAVIS
AND BRIAN JOHNSTON

D0112330

SUSAN C. MOORE, SERIES EDITOR

PLAYWRIGHTS in an hour
know the playwright, love the play
IN AN HOUR BOOKS • HANOVER, NEW HAMPSHIRE • INANHOURBOOKS.COM
AN IMPRINT OF SMITH AND KRAUS PUBLISHERS, INC • SMITHANDKRAUS.COM

With grateful thanks to Carl R. Mueller,
whose fascinating introductions to his translations of the Greek and
German playwrights provided inspiration for this series.

Published by In an Hour Books
an imprint of Smith and Kraus, Inc.
177 Lyme Road, Hanover, NH 03755
inanhourbooks.com SmithandKraus.com

Know the playwright, love the play.

In an Hour, In a Minute, and Theater IQ are registered trademarks of In an Hour Books.

Front cover design by Dan Mehling, dmehling@gmail.com
Text design by Kate Mueller, Electric Dragon Productions
Book production by Dede Cummings Design, DCDesign@sover.net

ISBN-13: 978-1-936232-16-1
ISBN-10: 1-936232-16-2
Library of Congress Control Number: 2009943214

CONTENTS

Why Playwrights in an Hour?

This new series by Smith and Kraus Publishers titled Playwrights in an Hour has a dual purpose for being: one academic, the other general. For the general reader, this volume, as well as the many others in the series, offers in compact form the information needed for a basic understanding and appreciation of the works of each volume's featured playwright. Which is not to say that there don't exist volumes on end devoted to each playwright under consideration. But inasmuch as few are blessed with enough time to read the splendid scholarship that is available, a brief, highly focused accounting of the playwright's life and work is in order. The central feature of the series, a thirty- to forty-page essay, integrates the playwright into the context of his or her time and place. The volumes, though written to high standards of academic integrity, are accessible in style and approach to the general reader as well as to the student and, of course, to the theater professional and theatergoer. These books will serve for the brushing up of one's knowledge of a playwright's career, to the benefit of theater work or theatergoing. The Playwrights in an Hour series represents all periods of Western theater: Aeschylus to Shakespeare to Wedekind to Ibsen to Williams to Beckett, and on to the great contemporary playwrights who continue to offer joy and enlightenment to a grateful world.

Carl R. Mueller
School of Theater, Film and Television
Department of Theater
University of California, Los Angeles

Introduction

Some playwrights are celebrated for their significance as builders, others for their power as breakers. Anton Chekhov, preeminently, seems to be refining the same play over and over again, exploring the same provincial setting, examining the same group of country characters. By contrast, the restless experimentation of August Strindberg, that self-declared "world incendiary," is devoted to perpetual transformation and change.

But it is very hard to catalogue the Norwegian playwright Henrik Ibsen in either category: he is both architect and revolutionary, builder and breaker. Often called the "father of modern drama," Ibsen not only creates a radically new theatrical technique called Modern Realism, he produces a series of explosive plays that, more than one hundred years after his death, continue to reverberate on our stages, tantalizing actors and directors as if they had been newly created.

True, Ibsen has been most widely known for the realistic contemporary dramas he developed out of the well-made plays of Eugène Scribe and Victorien Sardou during the 1870s and 1880s. Misinterpreted as "thesis" plays, which focus on a single theme, works such as *A Doll House* (written in 1879), *Ghosts* (written in 1881), and *The Wild Duck* (written in 1884) persuaded audiences that Ibsen's primary theatrical purpose was essentially social and domestic, dedicated to exposing bad marriages and corrupt institutions.

Although Ibsen always maintained a fierce rebellion against the smug conventions of those he called the "pillars of society," he always correctly held that "I have been more of a poet and less of a social philosopher than is commonly believed." The artist who first broke onto the world consciousness with groundbreaking plays like *Brand* (written in 1866), *Peer Gynt* (written in 1867), and *Emperor and Galilean* (written in

1873) was hardly the comfortable burgher once described by critic H. L. Mencken as "a highly respected member of the middle class, well-barbered, ease-loving, and careful in mind . . . a safe and sane exponent of order, efficiency, honesty, and common sense . . . [who] believed in all the things that the normal, law-abiding citizen of Christendom believes in, from democracy to romantic love, and from the obligations of duty to the value of virtue." Mencken was describing a man who was perhaps the most revolutionary dramatist who ever lived!

Ibsen's capacity to pursue a well-ordered domestic life while working to revolutionize the stage reminds us of Gustave Flaubert who once said you must be "regular and orderly in your life like a bourgeois so that you can be violent and original in your work." Ibsen, in exile from Norway for the first part of his life, certainly never neglected an opportunity to send shock waves through the community and, with his last semi-autobiographical plays — *The Master Builder* (written in 1892), *John Gabriel Borkman* (written in 1896), *When We Dead Awaken* (written in 1899) — even send shock waves through his own soul.

In his final plays, written toward the end of his life, he articulated his intention to enter the battlefield of artistic engagement again "with new weapons and in new armor." Modern drama would not have been the same without him. His spirit, his courage, and his fiery, modern vision shaped the century that followed his death.

Robert Brustein
Founding Director of the Yale and American Repertory Theatres
Distinguishing Scholar in Residence, Suffolk University
Senior Research Fellow, Harvard University

Ibsen

IN A MINUTE

AGE	DATE	
–	1828	**Enter Henrik Ibsen.**
1	1829	Chopin debuts in Vienna, Liszt proclaims him the best.
6	1834	The Spanish Inquisition, begun in 1478, is abolished by Isabella II.
11	1839	According to myth, Abner Doubleday organizes the first baseball game.
14	1842	Eugène Scribe — *The Glass of Water*
18	1846	Elias Howe invents the sewing machine.
20	1848	First U.S. women's rights convention in Seneca Falls, N.Y.
21	1849	Elizabeth Blackwell is first American woman to earn an M.D.
23	1851	*The New York Times* begins publishing on September 18.
26	1854	First railway opens in Norway between Oslo and Eidsvoll.
32	1860	Skiing becomes a competitive sport.
33	1861	Federal Fort at Sumter, South Carolina, surrenders to Confederate troops.
34	1862	Bismarck becomes prime minister of Prussia.
36	1864	Leo Tolstoy — *War and Peace*
38	**1866**	**Henrik Ibsen — *Brand***
39	**1867**	**Henrik Ibsen — *Peer Gynt***
42	1870	John D. Rockefeller founds Standard Oil Company.
43	1871	Charles Darwin — *The Descent of Man*
49	**1877**	**Henrik Ibsen — *Pillars of Society***
51	**1879**	**Henrik Ibsen — *A Doll House***
52	1880	Thomas Edison invents the electric lightbulb.
53	**1881**	**Henrik Ibsen — *Ghosts***
54	**1882**	**Henrik Ibsen — *An Enemy of the People***
55	1883	The Orient Express begins its run from Paris to Istanbul.
56	1884	Discovery of gold in South Africa leads to the rise of Johannesburg.
60	1888	August Strindberg — *Miss Julie*
64	1892	Oscar Wilde — *Lady Windermere's Fan*
73	1901	Anton Chekhov — *Three Sisters*
76	1904	A New York policeman arrests a woman for smoking a cigarette in public.
78	**1906**	**Exit Henrik Ibsen.**

A snapshot of the playwright's world. From historical events to pop-culture and the literary landscape of the time, this brief list catalogues events that directly or indirectly impacted the playwright's writing. The dates of Ibsen's plays are dates of publication. Many of his most important works made a huge impression on world literature and the theater when they were published, sometimes years before they ever reached the stage.

Ibsen

HIS WORKS

Ibsen often saw his plays published in book form long before they reached the stage, sometimes due to their controversial subject matter or their form and style. Therefore, the dates here are those of first publication.

EARLY PLAYS

Catiline (Catilina) (1850)

The Burial Mound (Kjæmpehøjen) (1850)

St. John's Eve (Sancthansnatten) (1852)

Lady Inger of Oestraat (Fru Inger til Østeraad) (1854)

The Feast at Solhaug (Gildet paa Solhoug) (1855)

Olaf Liljekrans (Olaf Liljekrans) (1856)

The Vikings at Helgeland (Hærmændene paa Helgeland) (1857)

MIDDLE PERIOD PLAYS

Love's Comedy (Kjærlighedens Komedie) (1862)

The Pretenders (Kongs-Emnerne) (1863)

Brand (Brand) (1866)

Peer Gynt (Peer Gynt) (1867)

The League of Youth (De unges Forbund) (1869)

Emperor and Galilean (Kejser og Galilæer) (1873)

This section presents a complete list of the playwright's works in chronological order. Titles appearing in another language indicate that they were first written and premiered in that language.

THE "PROSE CYCLE" OR "REALIST CYCLE" PLAYS

Pillars of Society (Samfundets støtter) (1877)

A Doll House (Et dukkehjem) (1879)

Ghosts (Gengangere) (1881)

An Enemy of the People (En Folkefiende) (1882)

The Wild Duck (Vildanden) (1884)

Rosmersholm (Rosmersholm) (1886)

The Lady from the Sea (Fruen fra havet) (1888)

Hedda Gabler (Hedda Gabler) (1890)

The Master Builder (Bygmester Solness) (1892)

Little Eyolf (Lille Eyolf) (1894)

John Gabriel Borkman (John Gabriel Borkman) (1896)

When We Dead Awaken (Når vi døde vågner) (1899)

SELECTED POETRY

Ibsen wrote poems (by the score) over his entire literary career, some of which have thematic connections to his major plays; a small selection of significant titles (dated by composition) follows.

"Resignation" (1847)

"Scandinavians Awake!" (1849)

"To Norway's Bards" (1850)

"Norma" (verse parody of Bellini's opera) (1851)

"The Miner" (1851)

"In the Picture Gallery" (1853)

"Wildflowers and Hothouse Plants" (1858)

"Mountain Life" (1859)

"On the Heights" (1859)

"To the Survivors" (1860)

"Terje Vigen" (1862)

"A Brother in Need" (1863)

"With a Water-lily" (1863)

"Gone" (1864)

"The Murder of Abraham Lincoln" (1865)

"To My Friend, the Revolutionary Orator" (1869)
"Thanks" (1871)
"Balloon-Letter to a Swedish Lady" (1871)
"A Letter in Rhyme" (1875)
"They Sat There, Those Two . . ." (1892)

ENGLISH TRANSLATIONS OF IBSEN'S POETRY

Lyrics & Poems from Ibsen. Translated by Fydell Edmund Garrett. New
York: E.P. Dutton & Co., 1912.

The Collected Poems of Henrik Ibsen. Translated by John Northam.
Available as a .pdf file:
http://ibsen.net/asset/34498/1/34498_1.pdf

VISUAL ART

According to the authoritative Norwegian Web resource, Ibsen.net:

"When Henrik Ibsen died, he left behind him a great many works in
the form of pictorial art: landscape paintings, cartoons, stage and costume sketches, and many more. In co-operation with Erik Henning Ed-
vardsen at the Ibsen Museum in Oslo, ibsen.net has produced a
database of all these works."

http://ibsen.net/index.gan?id=37400&subid=0 (July, 2007)

Onstage with Ibsen

Introducing Colleagues and
Contemporaries of Henrik Ibsen

 THEATER

Adolphe Appia, Swiss designer

Otto Brahm, German director

Anton Chekhov, Russian playwright and short story writer

Eleonora Duse, Italian actress

Eugène Scribe, French playwright

George Bernard Shaw, Irish playwright and essayist

Konstantin Stanislavsky, Russian actor and director

August Strindberg, Swedish playwright

 ARTS

Paul Gaugin, French painter

Charles Gounod, French composer

Edvard Grieg, Norwegian composer

Edouard Manet, French painter

Edvard Munch, Norwegian painter

Giacomo Puccini, Italian composer

Giuseppe Verdi, Italian composer

Richard Wagner, German composer

 FILM

Thomas Edison, American inventor

William Kennedy Laurie Dickson, American inventor of celluloid
    strip

Louis Aimé Augustin Le Prince, French inventor

Auguste and Louis Lumiere, French filmmakers

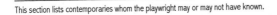
This section lists contemporaries whom the playwright may or may not have known.

Georges Melies, French filmmaker
Eadweard Muybridge, English photographer
Robert W. Paul, English inventor of film projector
Edwin S. Porter, American filmmaker

POLITICS/MILITARY

Otto von Bismarck, Prussian statesman
Benjamin Disraeli, British prime minister
Mahatma Gandhi, Indian leader
Oliver Wendell Holmes Jr., American jurist
Abraham Lincoln, American president
Karl Marx, German political and economic theorist
Napoleon III, French president and emperor
Queen Victoria, English monarch

SCIENCE

Marie Curie, Polish-French physicist
Charles Darwin, British naturalist
Albert Einstein, German physicist
Sigmund Freud, Austrian psychologist
Guglielmo Marconi, Italian inventor
Louis Pasteur, French biochemist
Max Planck, German physicist
Wilbur and Orville Wright, American inventors

LITERATURE

Hans Christian Andersen, Danish author
Charles Baudelaire, French poet
Charlotte and Emily Brontë, British novelists
Charles Dickens, British author
George Eliot, British novelist
James Joyce, Irish novelist
Leo Tolstoy, Russian author
Emile Zola, French author

RELIGION/PHILOSOPHY

Henry Ward Beecher, American minister

Henri Bergson, French philosopher

William James, American philosopher and psychologist

Søren Kierkegaard, Danish philosopher

John Stuart Mill, British philosopher

Cardinal Newman, Roman Catholic theologian

Friedrich Nietzsche, German philosopher

Herbert Spencer, British philosopher

SPORTS

Major W. C. Wingfield, British inventor of lawn tennis

Ty Cobb, American baseball player

John L. Sullivan, American boxer

Baron de Coubertin, French founder of the modern Olympics

William Muldoon, American wrestler

W. G. Grace, British cricketer

Tom Morris, Scottish golfer

James Naismith, Canadian-American inventor of basketball

INDUSTRY/BUSINESS

Karl Benz, German automotive engineer

Andrew Carnegie, Scottish-American industrialist and
philanthropist

George Eastman, American inventor

Henry Ford, American industrialist

William Randolph Hearst, American publisher

John Pierpont Morgan, American financier and industrialist

Alfred Nobel, Swedish arms manufacturer

George Pullman, American industrialist

IBSEN

in an
hour

> *"It may be questioned whether any man has held so firm*
> *an empire over the thinking world in modern times."*
> (James Joyce, 1900)

A REBEL IS BORN

In this brief comment, James Joyce confirms Henrik Ibsen's aston-
ishing progress from obscurity to world fame. Ibsen was born March
20, 1828, in Skien to Knud Ibsen and Marichen Altenburg. Skien, a
little Norwegian seacoast town, was on a remote fringe of Europe. At
the time, Norway was dominated politically by Sweden and culturally
by Denmark. Skien, with scarcely 3,000 inhabitants, lived off the
timber trade. Ibsen's mother was an avid painter and lover of theater.
She encouraged his artistic aspirations, and as a child, Ibsen had ambi-
tions to become a painter. Ibsen had a younger sister, Hedvig, and
three younger brothers, Johann Andreas , Nicolai Alexander, and Ole
Paus. He later had little contact with his younger brothers, two of

This is the core of the book. The essay places the playwright in the context of his or her world and analyzes the influences
and inspirations within that world.

whom emigrated to the United States (the third was to become a lighthouse keeper near Stavanger), but he corresponded with his sister.

Ibsen's father was a merchant whose fortunes ended in bankruptcy when Ibsen was eight years old. As a consequence, Ibsen was apprenticed at age fifteen to an apothecary in the even smaller town of Grimstad, some distance away. While there, he fathered an illegitimate son, whom he supported financially for a time, but he maintained no other contact with the child or his mother. He returned home only once in his life, for a brief visit in 1848. In his few spare hours from work he was an avid reader, particularly drawn to the French philosopher Voltaire. An inherently radical streak prompted the young Ibsen to write poems in support of the revolutions of 1848, then breaking out all over Europe, from the obscurity of Grimstad. This same radical temperament lay behind the choice of subject for his first play, *Catilina*, written while he lived in Grimstad. It *sympathetically* recounted the tragic career of the Roman rebel and criminal Catiline. In these first writings, we find what is to be a constant feature of Ibsen's career. He identified with the rebel, the outsider — the man or woman deeply alienated from conventional society.

This concept of *alienation* was a feature of the Romantic literature of Ibsen's early reading. He was among the first to give it a modern — and *modernist* — voice in the theater. There is a misconception of him as the troubled conscience of the conventional middle class, setting out to right its various wrongs. This misconception has prevented a broader recognition of his still remarkable daring as an imaginative artist. Instead, conventional theater histories tend to credit him more for laying the foundations of more exciting theatrical futures than for his own revolutionary work.

"MISUNDERSTOOD IN THE MIDST OF FAME"

One of the most persistent — and most limiting — misconceptions of Ibsen is that his plays are attempts to imitate everyday, "ordinary" real life in order to offer solutions to its problems. Ibsen's attitude toward the world in which he found himself was much more uneasy. It was closer at times to the apocalyptic visions of Dante's *Divine Comedy* or the satirical ire of Jonathan Swift than to the comfortably recognizable worlds of a playwright such as Arthur Miller. In a poem, he expressed regret he was not present at the time of the Ark with a torpedo! In letters, he professed to be an anarchist. The scale and uncompromising nature of his visionary art have eluded most commentators, who have settled for a more congenial version. A few characteristically fellow artists have detected its nature. The poet Rainer Maria Rilke, after seeing *The Wild Duck*, hailed Ibsen as "[a] new poet, whom we shall approach by many roads now that I know one of them. And again, someone misunderstood in the midst of fame."

Academic and socially driven interpretations have tended to harness Ibsen to a tamer agenda than he seems to have had in mind. These have reduced him to a wise old white-whiskered scold concerned only with correcting the errors of a troubled bourgeoisie. As Rilke commented: "A little while ago they were against you body and soul: and now they treat you as their equal. And they pull your words around with them in the cages of their presumption, and exhibit them in the streets, and tease them a little, from a safe distance. All your terrifying wild beasts."

Ibsen, thus tamed and domesticated, can neatly be slotted into anthologies of drama as "the father of modern realism." In the United States, he is mostly seen as the author of just two plays, *A Doll House* and *Hedda Gabler*. Yet his body of work includes such major verse plays as *Love's Comedy*, *Brand*, and *Peer Gynt*, as well as the historical dramas *The Pretenders* and *Emperor and Galilean*. He wrote twenty-eight plays.

He also wrote a sizeable catalogue of poetry, along with the essays, letters, and speeches typical of a nineteenth-century artist/intellectual.

The evolution of Ibsen's art underwent three decisive stages. First he wrote folkloric, mythic, and historical plays, mostly in verse. Then he had a "middle period" of plays not written for the theater. These included *Brand*, *Peer Gynt*, and *Emperor and Galilean*. In these plays he explored a huge dramatic universe in terms of expansive nature and the mythic-cultural past. Then he wrote a twelve-play cycle, containing his most famous prose plays, in which he infiltrates the previous dimensions into dramas of the modern world. This more expansive view of Ibsen's range makes it possible to acknowledge that his twelve so-called realistic plays (from *Pillars of Society*, 1877, to *When We Dead Awaken*, 1899) constitute an ambitious, interconnected cycle. These plays extend the realist method into mythic, historical, and archetypal dimensions, and they are as multilayered as the modernist work of T. S. Eliot or James Joyce.

A PAINTER WITH WORDS

Ibsen's early interest in painting is evident in his plays, which reveal a heightened sense of the visual possibilities of drama. The stage space serves as his canvas for creating a thoroughly "composed" and powerful theatrical iconography. Far more than most dramatists, he envisions the world of his plays completely. He incorporates powerful symbols — sometimes obvious, often very subtle. He also weaves patterns of visual imagery into the action. And these techniques are evident even at the very beginning of his long career.

He began writing his second play, the one-act *The Warrior's Barrow (Kjaempehøjen)*, while still in Grimstadt and completed it after moving to Christiania (now Oslo) in 1850. It was accepted and produced by the Christiania Theater that same year. He sold only a few copies of *Catilina*, but *The Warrior's Barrow* was performed three times. The play handles its huge subject — the conflict between paganism and Christianity — with considerable naiveté. It also exploits a theatrical device that will be of immense importance to the development not just of Ibsen's drama but of modern drama too. The action of the play centers on the onstage *visual symbol*. In this case, it is the Viking, masculine burial mound (barrow) recently strewn with flowers from a Christian and feminine hand. The flowers reveal the present at work on the past, as represented by the tomb of the pagan warrior. This painterly symbolic image encapsulates the pagan-Christian, masculine-feminine dialectic of the play. It is a contest between distant past and the present that continues all through Ibsen's work, making it his distinctive theme.

In his later plays, like *A Doll House*, Ibsen composes the entire stage set as a place of symbolic meaning and as an active realistic element of the drama. He uses meticulous stage directions, lighting, and props as ways of extending the metaphoric action. In a manner without real precedent in the modern tradition, the set becomes a major "actor" in an Ibsen play. The lighting creates atmosphere and emotion. The location of entrances suggests purposeful traffic patterns. The specific stage props are chosen with care so that they reinforce and extend the overall metaphoric intention of the play. These often lead to a moment of epiphany when the symbolic meaning flashes from the verbal and visual content.

The visual imagery of Ibsen's art is as important as verbal imagery is in Shakespeare's. Ibsen created a "poetry of the theater" for those modern plays in which he abandoned the verse medium and created modern realist drama. The stage space does not create just a plausible "setting" or milieu; it is a potent source of metaphors that are integral and active elements of the plot.

After *The Warrior's Barrow*, there is a decisive evolution and refinement of the visual elements of Ibsen's art. This reaches its climax in the final twelve-play Realist Cycle. The Ibsen realist stage set defines the cultural environment from which individuals derive their identities. For some characters (often the ones portrayed by Ibsen as less attractive or vigorous from an intellectual standpoint), these environments are comfortable enough. But for others (such as Nora in *A Doll House*, Hedda in *Hedda Gabler,* and Hilda and Solness in *The Master Builder*, to name but four), the carefully constructed world into which Ibsen places them causes them to suffer, rebel, and attempt to assert freer, more liberating, more adequate and authentic terms of action than the environments permit. They, then, invariably struggle to change their environment or, failing that, to escape it.

The scene too undergoes transformation and evolves along with the main characters. Ibsen's realistic stage sets, therefore, are not "backgrounds" to the action. They are composed to await — and help create — their epiphanies. These occur when the limiting and even repressive milieu suddenly displays submerged and subversive content and when the text opens up dimensions of reality beyond the restrictive mise en scène. Think of Nora's iconic slamming of the door at the end of *A Doll House* and how its finality as a symbolic sound effect stands for so much more than the story of a woman walking out on her husband and children. By this point in the drama, Ibsen has worked the visual and verbal (and in this case, sonic) imagery to such a climactic peak that the door can be understood as being slammed shut on an entire *world*.

BECOMING A MODERN DRAMATIST

When Ibsen moved in 1850 to the capital, Christiania, a city of about 30,000 inhabitants, he commenced a career that ultimately would lead to his long self-exile from Norway. It would also bring his gradual ascent to his major position in world literature. In Christiania, he joined with both learned and radical thinkers. He edited a student paper and wrote criticism of the drama performed in the capital.

Ibsen's initial motivation for the move to Christiania was to attend Christiania University, with the goal of becoming a physician. He first attended a "cram school" that prepared students for entering the university. Still, he failed to pass the entrance examinations to the university, coming up short in mathematics and Greek. It was at this point that he decided to devote himself to writing.

Native theater was practically nonexistent in Norway at the time. Danish companies performed plays from two major sources, France and Germany. Ibsen noted that the French drama, though technically accomplished, could not claim to be literature. He also indicated that German drama existed primarily as literature and only secondarily as theater. This was an extremely perceptive assessment of the two major traditions of the drama at the time, which were now reaching their end. One of Ibsen's main achievements in creating a modern drama was to unite these two features — theatrical effectiveness and literary quality. He joined them into a technically impressive *and* an intellectually ambitious modern dramatic art.

Until his first major play, *Love's Comedy*, in 1862, however, his apprenticeship was to be long and awkward. His early plays were exercises in the kind of Romantic poetic nationalism then current in Europe. These included *The Warrior's Barrow* (1850) through *The Vikings at Helgeland* (1858). He later repudiated them. For all their clumsiness, these early plays come across as the apprentice work of a large mind all the time exploring new dimensions of form and meaning.

One review he wrote at this time is particularly significant for understanding his later, multidimensional art. In this review, he defends the poet Frederik Paludan-Müller's use of ancient myths in his modern poems. Using terms borrowed from the German philosopher Hegel, Ibsen claims that mythic formulations originate in early consciousness, which transforms historical events into imaginative truths. These truths become part of folk consciousness (as Homer's poems were for the Greeks). Mythic thought, therefore, is embedded in a culture's collective identity. It can be drawn upon by artists as reference points connecting past and present, assisting those, like Ibsen, who seek to create a total "description of humanity."

In this, and in later writings, Ibsen argues for the multilayered nature of the cultural and the individual psyche, where past phases of human consciousness survive into the present. This was a major theme of all his drama. For example, the plays of the Realist Cycle resurrect, beneath their modern surfaces, archetypal themes, actions, and characters from our cultural heritage. In this, he anticipates the Modernist practice of Ezra Pound, T. S. Eliot, and James Joyce. The fascination of Ibsen's early writings lies in watching the way he gradually accumulates the many layers of his later dramatic technique.

Ibsen might well have been fortunate to fail his university entrance examination. This left him available, at the age of twenty-three, to accept the position of playwright-in-residence at the Norwegian Theatre in Bergen. It was newly founded by the eccentric genius Ole Bull, an internationally famous violinist who was also the founder of Oleanna, an ill-fated socialist-utopian community in the United States. The theater project was to prove more successful and more consequential for the world. It effectively launched Ibsen's career. Ibsen held this post for six years. It was during this period that Ibsen developed his theatrical acumen, as a writer, director, and producer of plays. He staged over 150 plays, as well as writing four plays based on Norwegian folklore and history. While in Bergen, Ibsen met Suzannah Thoresen, who would become his wife in 1858. Their only child, Sigurd (who later became a significant writer himself), was born in 1859. Ibsen formed a close friendship with Suzannah's stepmother, the novelist Magdalena Thoresen. She worked for him at the Bergen theater, translating plays from the French.

When Ibsen joined the Bergen theater in the 1850s, the standing of the theater in Europe was at a low point. This period witnessed the rise of the realistic novel as a major cultural force and the explosion of the Romantic movement in poetry and the arts. Yet hardly a single drama of major significance appeared. In the English-speaking world alone, it was the period of major poets. Wordsworth, Coleridge, Byron, Shelley, Keats, Tennyson, Browning, and Whitman were all writing. At the same time, Austen, the Brontës, Dickens, Eliot, Hawthorne, Melville, James, and Wharton were writing their novels. The same was true elsewhere.

The great period of German drama was over. No period since the Middle Ages was simultaneously so fertile in literature and so barren in drama. Many major authors attempted to write drama, but the theater ceased to be a significant cultural force. In England, the last play of any major literary and theatrical significance was Richard Brinsley Sheridan's *The School for Scandal* (1777). Then there was a drought of more than a century until the arrival in London of *A Doll House* in 1889, a decade after its original publication.

IBSEN'S THEATRICAL DNA: MELODRAMA AND THE WELL-MADE PLAY

The foundation for the modern theater was laid in Paris. After the revolution, that city witnessed a proliferation of theaters. These opened under a new law that allowed any citizen to start a theater company. The monopoly of the old royal theaters was over. Some thirty-six theaters sprang into being, offering everything from acrobatic and circus fare to sophisticated "well-made plays" and melodrama.

Under the influential melodramatist René-Charles Guilbert de Pixérécourt (1773–1844), melodrama in France became a theatrically spectacular genre, exporting to the rest of Europe and the United States. Melodrama created a world of spectacular natural effects. It portrayed a cosmos that took part in the human and moral drama. Earthquakes, storms, floods, fires, and collapsing buildings were some of the stage effects by which innocence was rescued and villainy astonishingly foiled. These were the visible equivalents of the divine interventions of earlier cultures. The sheer complexity of these effects — and their centrality to the dramaturgy of the plays — helped bring into being more sophisticated stage design practices.

THE WELL-MADE PLAY: CUSTOM-TAILORED FOR THE NEW BOURGEOISIE

Apart from the melodrama written for the masses, the other new form, directed toward the prosperous middle class, or bourgeoisie, was the well-made play. Its major practitioner, Eugène Scribe, wrote hundreds of such plays. He developed the form as sophisticated entertainment. The method behind the well-made play was to create the maximum of theatrical excitement by means of narrative energy with the minimum of intellectual or conceptual risk. This was an ideal form for the public of Paris under the Bourbon rulers and their censorship. The plot consisted of an intricate situation subjected to the pressure of urgent theatrical timing. Each act of the play contained a roller-coaster series of reversals and counterreversals. The party in whom the audience invested sympathy now was foiled, now was triumphant, only to be foiled again. The curtain fell on each act with the situation excruciatingly unresolved. In its cyclical rise and release of tension, it exploited the same kind of emotional interest as the stock exchange or gambling table.

The well-made play was continued by a number of playwrights, including Alexandre Dumas *fils*, Emile Augier, and Victorien Sardou. Like the melodrama, the well-made play was widely exported in the nineteenth century. It became the predominant form of the fashionable theater. Its basic structure remains influential today in Hollywood film scripts, television dramas, and popular theater.

The audience that assembled in the Parisian theaters was a miniature reconstruction of society. In the stalls and dress circles sat the well-to-do. In the next gallery, the middle-middle classes were found. In the top galleries were those better-off working classes who did not patronize the melodrama. To ensure the maximum revenue, all the social classes in attendance had to be kept contented, not divided into hostile factions. Ideas that encouraged critical thinking about society were kept off the stage. The managers simply could not afford to offend any section and lose its patronage.

Later came "thesis plays." These well-made plays took up some theme of topical social morality for a thoroughly conventional airing. For example, Alexandre Dumas *fils* in *La Dame aux camellias* (1848) created public scandal by the sentimental depiction of its courtesan heroine. The official censor allowed the play to be performed because the public commotion usefully distracted attention from the serious political and financial problems of the government in that turbulent year.

THEATER AS COMMODITY

The majority of the theatergoing public in belle-époque Paris included the wealthy patrons of the boulevard theaters. They were the smart, sophisticated, international patrons of operas, operettas, ballets, and well-made plays written to formulae. This was a public interested in undemanding entertainment. They definitely were not interested in complex "ideas" or any truly controversial subject matter. It was the period of large financial investments in the theater: in the buildings, sets, costumes, and star actors. Incurring such expenses, managers dared not risk alienating the public with controversial work. The only procedure for this new commodity theater was to play it safe. They stuck to the maxim "give the public what it wants." This was the advent of the entertainment industry.

There are enjoyable aspects of the well-made play. If nothing else, it provided safe entertainment for an intelligent and sophisticated public. The pleasure was to see the ingenious ways in which Eugène Scribe and his followers adapted the formulae to new subjects. Scribe would have been the first to admit his plays were just entertainments with no purpose behind them other than to be popular and profitable.

The well-made play lived up to its genre label. It was, at the very least, well made, and in Paris it was performed with a great deal of artistic skill. In *The Scenic Art*, Henry James, an avid theatergoer in Paris and London, was impressed by the Parisian product.

A good French play is an admirable work of art, of which it be-hooves patrons of the contemporary English drama, at any rate, to speak with respect. It serves its purpose to perfection, and French dramatists, as far as I can see, have no more secrets to learn. The first half-a-dozen a foreign spectator listens to seem to him among the choicest productions of the human mind, and it is only little by little that he becomes conscious of the extraordinary meagerness of their material. . . . Prime material was evidently long ago exhausted, and the best that can be done now is to re-arrange old situations with a kind of desperate ingenuity. The field looks terribly narrow, but it is still cleverly worked.

In other words, the French turned out a well-crafted commodity. This affected the whole way drama was discussed. Unlike the critics of earlier periods, who fought passionately over principles of dramatic art, there appeared a new class of critic. They served a public that wanted an evaluation of the craftsman's skill more than a consideration of the ideas or innovations of the artist. The nineteenth-century theater, therefore, was the last place in which to expect a visionary to appear. By 1850, Paris had fifty theaters. An even greater number outside France were willing to translate or adapt the plays. A well-made play, if successful, would be performed in numerous international venues and make a dramatist's fortune. This was a new development in dramatic art. A whole international network of theaters came into being to produce the latest product from Paris. This, in fact, was a valuable function of commodity theater: to keep up the profession, give it lots of work to do, and create a theatergoing public. It might be an essential function, for once this public is created, it is possible for the serious playwright to arrive and challenge it. Ibsen could not have become a world dramatist without the creation of an international theater public — a public that, if not ready to embrace him, at least was ready to be outraged, perplexed, and ultimately fascinated by him.

IBSEN VERSUS EVERYTHING: RECLAIMING THE THEATER

In 1857, Ibsen returned to Christiania to become creative director of the new Norwegian Theatre. After five years, the theater went bankrupt and closed, and Ibsen next went to work for the Christiania Theater. During this period he wrote *The Vikings of Helgeland*, *The Pretenders*, and *Love's Comedy*.

Ibsen, his wife, and son lived in difficult financial circumstances. Frustrated by the poor reception of his plays and the state of Norwegian theater, he emigrated to Sorrento, Italy, with his family in 1864. For the next twenty-seven years, Ibsen would remain abroad, living in Rome, Dresden, and Munich. It was during this self-imposed exile that Ibsen wrote his best-known works, among them *Brand* (1866), his first financially successful drama. In 1868, Ibsen moved to Dresden, where he spent the next five years writing his epic *Emperor and Galilean* (1873), dramatizing the life and times of the Roman emperor Julian the Apostate. In 1875, he moved to Munich, writing *A Doll House* (1879), which was followed by *Ghosts* in 1881.

Ibsen's volatile confrontation with the theater of his time is one of the ironies of cultural history. His identity as a dramatist seemed almost programmed to repudiate at every point the theatrical medium he was to dominate intellectually. He was continually rejected and assailed by the public. He was also reduced to poverty, ultimately choosing exile from Norway. Still, he doggedly worked upon the intractable theater of his time. He managed to forge a modern (and modernist) drama in his own revolutionary artistic vision. Even after his first major success with *Brand*, he kept up his adversarial stance toward the public. His resolve to make of the drama a major cultural force faced seemingly insuperable obstacles.

First, and fundamentally, there was no tradition of Norwegian drama. Its sole major dramatist, Ludvig Holberg (1684–1754), was dubbed "the Molière of the North." He left his native Bergen, and after traveling in Europe, he settled to live and work entirely in

Denmark. The stylistic awkwardness of Ibsen's earliest dramas occurs because he had to find his way with practically no native precedents. He built up from scratch both the subject matter and the form of a modern Norwegian dramatic art. Current dramatic genres and styles from outside Norway existed, but they had to be unlearned, reformed, or outgrown.

Ibsen compared directing Scribe's plays at the Bergen theater to committing "daily abortions." The German tradition of historical drama was a more decisive influence. *Catilina* owes an obvious debt to Schiller's equally youthful and rebellious *The Robbers (Die Räuber)*. In addition, Ibsen's series of historical dramas that culminate in *Emperor and Galilean* draws on the Germanic tradition's profound link between philosophy and drama. This began with Lessing's *Nathan the Wise (Nathan der Weise*, 1779). Goethe's *Faust* (1808–32) clearly influenced *Peer Gynt*.

By the time he inaugurated his Realist Cycle with *Pillars of Society* (1877), Ibsen had evolved a formidable mastery of his medium. His mastery went far beyond the technical skills of the French boulevard playwrights. He demonstrated it convincingly with a virtuoso transcendence of their methods in *Hedda Gabler*. There he employed a vast, even epic array of philosophically influenced subject matter — including the world-historical conflict between pagan and Christian worldviews. This he cunningly compressed into the shapely confines of the boulevard dramatic form, with its intricate plotting and series of surprises. Instead of exploiting his mastery of this facility for commercial success, however, he chose the decidedly nonlucrative path of artistic integrity. Michael Meyer, in his biography of Ibsen, estimates that even at the height of his fame in the decade following *A Doll House* (a span that included such major works as *Ghosts, An Enemy of the People, The Wild Duck, Rosmersholm, The Lady from the Sea*, and *Hedda Gabler*) he earned less than a fashionable dramatist would make in a single year.

"MORE THE POET": IBSEN'S ENCOUNTER WITH MODERN LIFE

Ibsen rejected both ingratiating representations of modern reality and the writing of plays that addressed easily identifiable social problems in need of reform. In his speech to the Norwegian League for Women's Rights in 1898, which is printed in *Ibsen: Letters and Speeches*, he remarked, "I have been more the poet and less the social philosopher than is commonly believed. My task has been the description of humanity." He was enlisted by social reformers to their causes and has been interpreted in that light ever since. This is how he continues to be "misunderstood in the midst of fame," as Rilke observed. Far from being benevolently reform-minded, his art performs an act of cultural demolition in the Nietzschean mode. He attacks the fundamental beliefs on which our civilization is founded. The clue to Ibsen's procedure in the Realist Cycle is the launching of an inexorable dialectical process. In this process, a *thesis* (such as Nora's happy marriage) reveals its inherent contradictions and is destroyed, creating the *antithesis*. This leads to a *synthesis* (a search for a new basis of marriage), and the process is taken up again in another work with a new thesis. In Ibsen, this dialectic struggle describes the still-incomplete development of human consciousness, institutions, and societies. As it unfolds, from beginning to end of the cycle, it corrodes and destroys the whole fabric of our assumed reality.

The dialectic gives to Ibsen's plays their devastating dynamic. Ibsen's advocates insisted his plays needed a new kind of presentation. They advocated for a new kind of acting to do justice to their revolutionary form. In his critical writings, George Bernard Shaw insisted on the complete unsuitability of the old acting style for the "new drama." This theme was taken up by Ibsen's translator William Archer and by Elizabeth Robins in *Ibsen and the Actress* (1928). The tremendous care with which Ibsen texts were translated and prepared for performance in London represented a dedication entirely new in the theater. This was despite pitifully impoverished means and for runs often of no more than two or three days. There was great respect for the author's intentions. A critical tradition evolved to introduce, champion, and interpret the plays in the face of an unremittingly hostile critical reception. All this constituted a collaborative discipline between scholars, interpreters, performers, and enthusiasts. This stood in stark contrast to the cavalier indifference to texts displayed by the traditional theater profession. Ibsen's plays were recognized as artistic unities to whose integrity productions should be faithful. According to Henry James, in *The Scenic Art*, in 1891, this conscientiousness was richly rewarded, not financially but aesthetically.

> . . . [T]he author of *The Pillars of Society* and of *The Doll's House*, of *Ghosts*, of *The Wild Duck*, of *Hedda Gabler*, is destined to be adored by the 'profession.' (He) will remain intensely dear to the actor and the actress. He cuts them out work to which the artistic nature in them joyously responds — work difficult and interesting, full of stuff and opportunity. The opportunity that he gives them is almost always to do the deep and delicate thing — the sort of chance that, in proportion as they are intelligent, they are most on the look out for. ("On the Occasion of *Hedda Gabler*" in *The Scenic Art*, p. 245.)

If the artistic satisfactions were rich, the financial rewards were meager. Productions of Ibsen plays were comparatively rare. When they occurred they were often runs of one or two weeks at the most, under impoverished conditions, at unfashionable locations and hours. "Considering how much Ibsen has been talked about in England and America he has been lamentably little seen and heard," complained Henry James in 1891. However, a cultural "space" was now emerging that was independent of the London commercial scene and its moralizing censorship.

Though little seen and heard, he was heatedly discussed. At first the controversy centered upon the "moral aspect" of Ibsen's art. Henry

James commented on this feature of the controversy. In the review of *Hedda Gabler* cited above, he noted "those cries of outraged purity which have so often and so pathetically resounded through the Anglo-Saxon world." The controversy reached fever pitch in London on Friday, March 13, with the single performance of *Ghosts*, at J. T. Grein's "Independent Theatre." This was a private club brought into being to circumvent the censorship that banned public performances of the play — a ban that stayed in effect in Britain for nearly thirty years. George Bernard Shaw wrote, in Dramatic Opinions and Essays, of the press reaction to the production:

> There was one crowded moment when, after the first performance of "Ghosts," the atmosphere of London was black with vituperation, with threats, with clamor for suppression and extinction, with everything that makes life worth living in modern society. (*Dramatic Opinions*, p. 55)

Despite the almost universal outrage expressed in the London press, it now became apparent that a minority public was evolving. It was hungry for a theater into which one could take one's intellect. This partly accounts for the success of Ibsen with the "thinking world" when his plays began to appear on the European stage. Ibsen Societies (of the Left and Right) were formed to pronounce Ibsen the Prophet of a New Revelation. The "Ibsen phenomenon" spread to the rest of the continent and to the Americas. His plays were hailed as inaugurating a new drama. The task of defending them against hostile commentary gave rise to a new criticism. It notably raised the level of discourse on dramatic art. It meant defending and explaining the nature of the plays and becoming familiar with their baffling procedures. Ibsen's British translator, William Archer, commented in 1891 on the interest in Ibsen:

> His name is in every newspaper and magazine, his rankling phrases . . . are in every mouth. . . . This is the first time for

half a century (to keep well within the mark) that a serious
literary interest has also been primarily a theatrical interest.
(in Michael Meyer, *Ibsen*, p. 659)

A sophisticated interpretation of modern drama now emerged.
Soon the adherents of the conventional theater found themselves
obliged to defend their own preferences against the new critics. To
perform this new drama to its admirers, minority theaters came into
being in Berlin (the Freie Bühne, 1889) and London (the Independent
Theatre, 1891). They were formed specifically to perform Ibsen's
Ghosts. They were the cradles of serious modern drama. In Paris,
André Antoine's Théâtre Libre was founded in 1887. It performed
Ghosts in 1890. George Moore was so moved by the play he became a
founding member of a new Irish Literary Theatre — later to become
Ireland's Abbey Theatre.

ALL THE WORLD, HIS STAGE

Ibsen, it could be argued, was the first world dramatist. In the latter
part of his career, he was the first dramatist conscious of addressing
a world audience rather than a national one. As soon as his plays
appeared, in print or onstage, they were major cultural events in many
countries. Of William Archer's translation of *John Gabriel Borkman*,
George Bernard Shaw, with admittedly Shavian hyperbole, declared:

Already Ibsen is a European power: this new play has been
awaited for two years, and is now being discussed and assimi-
lated into the consciousness of the age with an interest which
no political or pontifical utterance can command. . . . Ibsen is
translated promptly enough nowadays, yet no matter how
rapidly the translation comes on the heels of the original,
newspapers cannot wait for it: detailed accounts based on the
Norwegian text, and even on stolen glimpses of the proof-
sheets, fly through the world from column to column as if

the play were an Anglo-American arbitration treaty. (*Dramatic Opinions*, p. 158)

With the Ibsen phenomenon, theater and drama now joined the other arts of the modern world in addressing separate, and often mutually hostile, mainstream and minority publics. Public performances of *Ghosts* were banned in Europe. In England, the ban would last for twenty-three years! Reviewers in the popular press greeted each new play with hostility. Mainstream criticism resembled the outrage greeting the work of Charles Baudelaire, Gustave Flaubert, and Emile Zola. It also resembled the reception accorded to Edouard Manet and the Impressionist painters. Theater managers did not welcome this development. After all, they had been pursuing the highly lucrative policy of appealing to all levels of society in their audiences. They were as anxious as the government censors to keep out controversial and socially divisive drama.

But Ibsen's plays were not only controversial. They also were aesthetically compelling, capable of luring a discriminating minority away from the mainstream theater. Gradually, the ranks of this discriminating public increased. But until this happened, a striking contrast persisted between Ibsen's intellectual success in the cultural life of Britain and Europe and the very meager commercial rewards. However, this lack of financial reward actually made Ibsen more indispensable in bringing about the new drama. Few dramatists in the countries where his plays were introduced could have survived on such modest returns. Yet without the drama he brought into being in the minority theater, there would have been no consistently compelling work to present and no gradually emerging public receptive to it. The future of serious modern drama lay with Ibsen and his determined pursuit of his art.

Performing an Ibsen play was considered virtually an insurrectionary act. Ibsen became the most vilified, championed, talked and written about individual in Europe. Divisions appeared even in the ranks of Ibsen's champions. For example, he was differently perceived in Britain and France. The almost "exclusively moral" emphasis of "Anglo-Saxon" commentary was noted by Henry James and others. This meant that in Britain, Ibsen's plays were seen primarily as trenchant criticisms of contemporary life. As a consequence, the plays were praised for their *realism*, while their symbolic and aesthetic qualities mostly were ignored.

In France, the Théâtre Libre's naturalist interpretations of Ibsen began to give way to a new vision of the plays. They seemed to belong to the Symbolist movement, in the manner of Maurice Maeterlinck. Lugné-Poe's Théâtre de l'Oeuvre, founded in Paris in 1893, enlisted Ibsen in the ranks of the Symbolists. According to Pascal Casanova, for a production of *The Lady from the Sea*, Lugné-Poe "inaugurated a new style of acting, solemn and monotone, whose emphasis on speaking lines slowly . . . had the effect of making the text seem unreal." When he brought his interpretations to Scandinavia, the critical reception was generally favorable. Ibsen himself was pleased. Shaw gave qualified praise for the Théâtre de l'Oeuvre's production of *Peer Gynt* in Paris in 1896. Lugné-Poe later reined in the extravagant excesses of his Symbolist effects and settled for a more realistic performance style. Yet the perception of Symbolist dimensions to Ibsen's art provided a welcome corrective to the relentlessly "realistic" (and often moralistic) emphasis of "Anglo-Saxon" commentary.

Ibsen, therefore, either as realist or symbolist, offered a drama that was in tune with the leading ideas and artistic achievements of the time. The new minority public was a highly critical, often rebellious intelligentsia. It was variously at odds with the aesthetic, moral, political, and religious premises of conventional society. Ibsen's dramas addressed these levels of cultural alienation. Henry James, Thomas Hardy, George Moore, Oscar Wilde, George Bernard Shaw, and James Joyce were among the many who took up his cause. They were joined by the progressive men and women of Europe and, later, the United States. They supported the new independent theater movement his plays inaugurated. He was most appreciated in the German-speaking world. Gerhart Hauptmann, Rainer Maria Rilke, Thomas Mann, Hugo von Hoffmansthal, Sigmund Freud, and (more ambivalently) Frank Wedekind were among his admirers.

WHO AM I? A NEW ERA LOOKS AT CHARACTER

The dominant middle class of the nineteenth century was riddled with contradictions. It was as tragic — or comic — as any in history. The intellectual world was post-Darwinian. Its social structure was industrial-capitalist, and its policies emphatically pragmatist. It proclaimed traditional moral values. But it was notably unwilling to acknowledge the sources and consequences of its materialism, which made a mockery of both its idealism and its morality. It was uncertain of its biological or cultural identity, its history, or its destiny.

Most art and public discourse supplied a reassuring image. It was based on firmly conventional values in formulations the public gratefully consumed. Hjalmar Ekdal, in *The Wild Duck*, "retouching" photographic reality, is a portrait of the type. Many thinkers, however, were deeply uneasy about the discrepancy between these flattering images and the grim realities that contradicted them. In response, a revolution in sensibility in all the arts took place. In literature, this led to a radical rethinking of the human condition.

Earlier tragic characters in drama, from Sophocles' Ajax to Racine's Phèdre, agonized over the threat to their *integrity*. However, the tragic dilemma of Romantic and post-Romantic characters can be stated as loss of *authenticity*. This was not a concern with being true to one's identity. Rather it was an existential doubt as to whether one *has* an identity to be true to. This is exemplified by Ibsen's Peer Gynt, who can ask:

Was I ever myself? Where, whole and true?
Myself, with God's seal stamped on my brow?

The terror of nonidentity and the anxiety over authenticity are driving forces of Ibsen's drama. In *A Doll House*, it brings Nora Helmer to realize she knows neither the world she lives in nor her own identity in it. Gregers Werle, of *The Wild Duck*, sees his "mission" as the rescue of the Ekdal family. He perceives the family as trapped in a swamp of inauthenticity. It is presided over by his manipulative father and Dr. Relling, a dispenser of illusion-sustaining false identities ("life-lies"). The same anxiety fuels Hedda Gabler's simmering resentment at the role assigned her in the "absurd" world she finds closing around her. It urges Master Builder Halvard Solness to recover and replay one genuinely authentic, supremely self-willed action: his ascent, against all his innate fears, of a tall spire he has built, in a challenge to the "Creator."

Ibsen's plays uncover abysses of unreality concealed beneath the reality we imagine we inhabit. They are not concerned with merely airing some social problem to be put right, as many of Ibsen's admirers insist in a misguided effort to tame and domesticate his art. As early as 1907, Jennette Lee protested against this still prevalent interpretation. She said, "The conception of a problem play as one in which some problem of modern life is discussed by the characters and worked out in the plot is foreign to Ibsen, as to all great artists."

Nineteenth-century culture was riven with contradictions that it debated fiercely and openly. It was a time of political and intellectual emancipation. Many peoples struggled for independence from foreign rule. At the same time, it was the age of cynical colonial imperialism in the Middle East, Africa, and the Far East. It was also the time of the dispossession and annihilation of the native inhabitants of North America. In the arts, there was a dynamism in form and subject matter rarely seen before. At the same time, the proliferation of popular commodity culture represented a total collapse of any fine sense of form or taste. There were stirrings of universal suffrage, unparalleled advances of knowledge, prosperity, and science. At the same time, huge cities were created with their hideous slums and the exploited proletariat living and working in inhuman conditions. Ibsen, in *Brand*, inveighed against "the hideous smoke stacks" polluting the natural world. Modern humanity was markedly more rapacious, destructive, and violent than the conventional moral and religious ideals its arts and pieties proclaimed. As the Old Man of the Dovre tells Peer Gynt:

> You human creatures are all of a kind.
> In your speech it's all 'spirit' that governs your deeds;
> But you count on your fists to take care of your needs.

THE PRESENCE OF THE PAST: ARCHETYPES IN IBSEN

Ibsen's aim, like that of every major poet, was to liberate our *imaginations* by revealing a more *adequate* idea of ourselves and of our world. Liberation from self-deception meant identifying the forces in the historical past that make us what we are: those inherited forces and powers that both drive our conflicts and set limits to our capacity for freedom.

The past is always ambiguously present in Ibsen's modern plays. On the one hand, it is a malign power imprisoning our souls, encouraging the lethal throwbacks that still plague us. These resemble the "received ideas" of Gustave Flaubert's *Dictionary of Received Ideas (Le Dictionnaire des Idées Reçues)* — slovenly habits that replace genuine thinking. But there is something that goes deeper: the past that "walks again" as perceived by Helene Alving in *Ghosts*:

> The dead among us — ghosts. . . . I almost believe we are ghosts, all of us. It's not just what we inherit from our fathers and mothers that walks again in us — it's all sorts of dead old ideas and dead beliefs and things like that. They don't exactly *live* in us, but there they sit all the same and we can't get rid of them. All I have to do is pick up a newspaper, and I see ghosts lurking between the lines. I think there are ghosts

everywhere you turn in this country — as many as there are grains of sand — and then there we all are, so abysmally afraid of the light.

But there are benign ghosts, also. Human evolution leaves behind a trail of values and achievements, forgotten or suppressed, that still might be reclaimed for the benefit of the future. Perceiving that aspects of our humanity are violently in conflict — as in the clash between humanist and religious identities, our rational and spiritual needs — Ibsen envisioned a union of these antitheses into a new synthesis of human wholeness. In his mammoth ten-act drama *Emperor and Galilean*, he termed this sought-after union a "third empire of the spirit." Variations of the quest for this synthesis, this "third way," have occupied writers and thinkers from the Renaissance and the Enlightenment through to the present day.

Realism was an extension of the Romantic movement. From Romanticism came the conviction that society and its conventions are forms of "false consciousness," of "alienation" that stood in the way of achieving our free and full humanity. The purpose of art was not to imitate this false reality but to create an alternative imaginative space. There it might be possible to discover a more adequate human identity.

"Art reveals life to us as it should be," wrote Ibsen's son, Sigurd. "If the natural process that life is, for the most part, could ever be organized in such a way that existence should be recreated in the image of humanity, then art would be superfluous: for life itself would have become art." Present life, that is, is a defective work of art, a disfigurement of the "image of humanity," which a true artist must seek to restore or re-create.

Characters and actions in Ibsen's realist plays are not only compelling representatives of our modern world. They are, as importantly, vessels or representatives of cultural forces whose conflicts go back centuries. By creating a realist method where different historical and cultural levels continuously intersect, Ibsen anticipated a major principle of modernism. Ezra Pound, T. S. Eliot, and James Joyce worked with these same principles. Ibsen produced the literary equivalent of the intersecting spatial perspectives of, for example, Cubism in painting. This realist method reveals the *unreality* of the familiar-seeming modern life it purports to be presenting. The solid seeming "modernity" of his stage dissolves to reveal more adequate archetypal presences.

The recurrent action in Ibsen's modern plays, therefore, consists of two strategies: (1) A dialectical action that reveals the contradictions in modern reality, and (2) the infiltration of more adequate, archetypal dimensions of reality.

THE DIALECTICAL DIMENSION

The *dialectics* of Ibsen's drama derive from his Romantic heritage. In both dramas and philosophical writings, for example, the great German playwright/poet Friedrich von Schiller depicted his culture in terms of dialectics: between enlightenment and reaction, "naive and sentimental," bringers of light and powers of darkness. In such plays as *Don Carlos* and *Mary Stuart*, the characters onstage stand for opposing, even antithetical historical/cultural forces. These forces tragically fail to arrive at more adequate, "higher" syntheses — in the manner of classical drama.

Ibsen continued this dialectical procedure. He transferred it from the historical scenes of his own earlier plays into the images of his modern realist method. This method does not set out to imitate everyday reality but to demolish it. Each play in the twelve-play Realist Cycle sets forth a dialectical action where the thesis and the antithesis collide, creating a synthesis that leaves a void, an implosion, often a question for the next play in the cycle to address.

In an Ibsen play, the dialectic shapes the plot: The action of each play totally reverses the conditions of its opening premises. The first four plays of the Realist Cycle show how each plot enforces a dialectical reversal of situation. In *The Pillars of Society*, a self-congratulatory moral community is revealed as a society of lies needing to know itself for the first time. The heroine of *A Doll House* evolves from a conventional housewife into a social rebel. Her sustaining home is exposed as a spiritual prison. *Ghosts* begins with a fraudulent memorial to an exemplary father and citizen set up by his self-justifying wife, who secretly resents his crime against her. It ends by demolishing all the memorial stands for as the father's true identity is acknowledged and honestly honored by the wife condemning her crime against him. In *An Enemy of the People*, the hero begins as a proclaimed savior and patriot rescuing his community from physical danger. His home is a center of hospitality. Later he is transformed into the enemy of the community. He and his house are attacked and reviled. He finds himself provoked into launching a campaign against his community's spiritual ills. The world of each play, which seemed so assuredly safe, known, and solid at the outset, implodes and turns out to be fragile, unknown, and even dangerous.

A dramatic plot is usually a means of presenting the information necessary to know the story of a play. Sometimes it provides the thrilling artifices of the theater. This is true in the well-made-play format. The plot of an Ibsen play is the dialectic at work reshaping "bad" reality into a form that reveals what everyday reality has turned its back on. The information the plot seems to be providing turns out not to be trustworthy even though the characters who give the information believe they are telling the truth.

This is probably what still perplexes audiences about Ibsen. Dialectical thinking is unnerving. For Ibsen, however, dialectical conflict, tearing apart the fabric of "known" reality, is the healthy condition of the spirit. It is not the destructive disorder that appalled the Shakespearean worldview. All that the Shakespearean drama considered natural and good — order, hierarchy, established tradition — is seen instead as unnatural, intolerably constraining, standing in the way of self-determination. And this brings about a total change in all the main elements of drama: *scene*, *character*, *action*, and *dialogue*.

IBSEN'S METHOD IN ACTION

By looking at *A Doll House*, we can learn about the method of all the plays. First, the *scene*: the pleasant, tastefully furnished Helmer home and its assured place in its community will be exposed as a realm of unreality, of false consciousness. Ibsen's realistic method specifies a stage set that dictates the scale and type of the action that will unfold. He gives the details of furniture and costumes. He also gives the stage directions for the gestures of the actors and even, at times, the pitch of their voices. This realistic milieu already determines the limits of what can plausibly be said and done within the setting. Devices like asides, soliloquies, impenetrable disguises, and violent or extravagant actions won't work in this setting. The stabbings, duels, and carnage of Elizabethan theater with their extravagant histrionics would immediately be perceived as incongruous. Realism's demand for recognizable situations and behaviors makes it harder for the artist who is trying to tell stories and grapple with ideas that transcend the world of the every day. Ibsen's aesthetic vision is uniquely suited to the task of rendering "a great reckoning in a little room." That is, he manages the artistic sleight-of-hand of embedding large, multi-dimensional actions and ideas within stories and settings that the audience accepts as plausible and human scaled.

Yet even in this ostensibly realistic setting, Ibsen infuses the stage with potent scenic images that help unravel the worn fabric of conventional society. Take, for example, the Christmas tree (a pagan custom adopted by later Christian cultures) that will stand as mute commentator on this holiday's unexpected turn. Look also at the piano, which might seem to be a harmless bourgeois nicety but becomes the instrument by which Nora's tarantella dance reaches a frenzied climax that Torvald criticizes as "too naturalistic." Then there is the carefully placed door through which Krogstad insinuates himself into the Helmer household and through which Nora makes her cataclysmic final exit, which Shaw famously called "the door slam heard round the world."

The plays use *characters* in a similar way. The social order that designates the characters of Torvald as a pillar of society and Nils Krogstad as a social outcast is based on a false idea of reality. This false idea is one that is held by most in Ibsen's audience too. When Torvald declares "I literally feel sick when I'm around someone like [Krogstad]," he unwittingly reveals the irony that he is living off the moral as well as financial credit advanced by Krogstad. Indeed Krogstad performs the convenient role of moral villain by which Torvald can define himself as moral pillar.

The separation of humanity into mutually exclusive moral categories — the good and the bad, easily recognized and defined — is exposed as a conventional but lethal fiction. Ibsen's dialectical plotting employs an art of *estrangement* by which, bit by bit, the image of reality on the stage reveals its actual *unreality*. It is a subtler action of estrangement (or alienation) than Bertolt Brecht's is. But it is equally devastating, as the tumultuous reception of Ibsen's plays revealed. To have one's whole idea of reality gradually and relentlessly demolished in front of one's eyes is an alarming theatrical experience, perhaps just as alarming as having one's idea of reality directly assaulted.

Under the pressure of events (*action*) the charming and reassuring Helmer home changes. It becomes, in the evolving consciousness of the main character, Nora, first suddenly fragile, needing to be desperately defended. Then it changes to an unbearable prison of inauthenticity from which she flees to search for her own identity and the nature of the world she inhabits. As she undergoes this evolution, the *dialogue* also evolves. Her language's imagery and key terms change as she discards false concepts and evolves new ones.

This happens to the other characters as well. Krogstad, for

example, begins the play in what appears to be almost a stereotypical melodramatic villain's role, bringing the threat of destruction to the happy Helmer household. His language is full of legal terms designed to corner Nora in the admission of her crime, the forgery of her father's signature to secure a loan with which to save Torvald's life. By Act Three, however, Krogstad has taken on some of the attributes of a romantic hero. He and Kristine Linde, lovers parted by years of bitter necessity, reunite. Krogstad's last action — from offstage, through the letter box — offers the Helmers the return of the note he earlier had planned to use to blackmail them.

In a conventional well-made play, the note's return would trigger the rush to a "happy ending" and a quick, ecstatic final curtain. But Ibsen is once again embedding a larger action, a bigger notion, within what seems like a comfortable frame. As Torvald reads Krogstad's message, his elation is barely containable. He cries out that they are "saved," that he "forgives" Nora, offers his "broad wings" to "shelter" her from the hard world outside.

Nora's response, however, is not to run to his arms like the guilty wife of a boulevard drama as the curtain falls. Instead she goes into her room to change out of her party costume and into her traveling clothes. When she reenters, Ibsen's dialectical method reaches the moment of *synthesis*, as Nora demolishes the premises on which her marriage had been built and leaves only an impossible question in their place.

Here, Ibsen's command of the language of the stage reaches its highest expression. He endows a single word, repeated purposefully in each act, with the ability to carry the thesis-antithesis-synthesis structure of the entire dialectic. Observe the evolution of the meaning of the key term *wonderful* in the three acts. To ensure it registers as a key term, in each act it is sounded three times in succession. In Act One, the "wonderful" represents objective material happiness — literally having enough money to be comfortable and secure. In Act Two, "wonderful" is a subjective romantic fiction of Nora and Torvald's mutual heroism, in which she imagines them both committing great deeds under pressure. This is almost as though it were a melodrama or a Romantic poem. Finally, in Act Three, it is sounded as a call for a new form of human existence, requiring a new definition of marriage, of honesty and truth.

And the dialectic is irreversible. There can be no going back to a previous phase of consciousness. The Nora of Act Two has journeyed irrevocably far from the Nora of Act One, and she is evolving the equally irreversible consciousness of the Nora of Act Three. Torvald, too, at the end, no longer inhabits the same world, speaks the same language, or is the same person as in Act One. Ibsen's theater brings to the Helmers, at this time of Christmas, the devastating gifts of truth and freedom that "everyday" life is designed to deny. (Many translations miss the dialectic and alternate "the wonderful" with "the miracle." This deprives the text of a purposeful poetic pattern as well as the all-important dialectical evolution of a concept.)

Dialectic, the process by which situations are forced to reveal, and overcome, their inherent contradictions, is the pulse beat of the whole twelve-play Realist Cycle. It drives its inexorable sequence of imploding and evolving actions from the first play, *Pillars of Society*, to the last, *When We Dead Awaken*. At first sight, these two plays are totally different in both subject and dramatic method. Viewed side by side in isolation, they seem to be written by radically different dramatists. But Ibsen insisted on "the mutual connections between the plays." He added: "Only by grasping and comprehending my entire production as a continuous whole will the reader be able to conceive the precise impression I sought to convey in the individual parts of it. I therefore appeal to the reader that he not put any play aside . . . experiencing them intimately in the order in which I wrote them." If we do, we will see how *Pillars of Society* and *When We Dead Awaken* are linked in a single, evolutionary chain. The last play could not exist — and cannot be understood — without the first. This is the imaginative voyage Ibsen invites us to share with him.

LAST ACT

In July 1891, Ibsen journeyed from Munich to Norway, intending to spend a long summer holiday in his native country. He returned home as a world-famous, though controversial, playwright and to a Norway much changed from the one he left. His countrymen entreated him to resume his residence in Norway, and he settled in Christiania. On his seventieth birthday, in 1898, the world paid him homage, with representatives of various theaters and academic and state bodies visiting him all day. A group of admirers in England, which included Thomas Hardy and George Bernard Shaw, sent him a set of silver plate to commemorate the day. Ibsen continued to write until 1900, when he suffered the first of several strokes that would afflict him over the next years. On May 23, 1906, he passed away in Christiania after a series of strokes. When his nurse assured his family, standing nearby, that he was a little better, Ibsen reputedly said, "To the contrary," and then died. Ibsen was buried in Vår Frelsers graylund (The Graveyard of Our Savior) in central Oslo.

DRAMATIC MOMENTS

from the Major Plays

These short excerpts are from the playwright's major plays. They give a taste of the work of the playwright. Each has a short introduction in brackets that helps the reader understand the context of the excerpt. The excerpts, which are in chronological order, illustrate the main themes mentioned in the In an Hour essay.

Six Final Scenes

The way a playwright ends a work is always significant. In the ending, a play often reveals its worldview. Who wins, who loses? Does Miss Prism's famous summary of poetic justice (from Wilde's *The Importance of Being Earnest*) prevail: "The good ended happily, and the bad unhappily. That is what Fiction means" or are there more nuanced outcomes? Is there even such a thing as poetic justice in the world of the play? Who, or what, if anything, seems to be in charge? Endings focus our attention on questions such as these.

Throughout his career, Ibsen proved to be an innovator in his final scenes, typically rejecting both the classical tradition of restoring order and the nineteenth-century plot-driven concept of the *denouement*, or the "untying of the knot." Ibsen's endings have both theatrical and thematic effect: Think of the avalanches that carry both *Brand* (1866) and his last play, *When We Dead Awaken* (1899), to their surprising conclusions. In both cases, an absolute force of nature sweeps away human absolutes (religious in the former play, artistic/spiritual in the latter). Yet, the endings themselves are far from absolute; they are, instead, profoundly open, even enigmatic, leaving room for the next set of questions to emerge in the world's continuously evolving consciousness.

For our selected excerpts from Ibsen's plays, we have chosen to look at the final scenes from *Peer Gynt*, *A Doll House*, *Ghosts*, *Hedda*

Gabler, The Master Builder, and *When We Dead Awaken.* Each of them is built around a significant event — a departure, or in the case of *Peer Gynt*, a return — that changes the world of the play and casts shadows beyond, into the culture at large. Ibsen, instead of providing his characters (and his audience) with an easy, extractable theme or moral, insists on closing in the interrogative mood, on a note of question. He will vary this pattern throughout his career, but the consistent feature of his endings is their simultaneous function as *beginnings* of the next part of the conversation Ibsen wants to have with the world. Here, then, are endings (and beginnings) from six of Ibsen's greatest works.

from **Peer Gynt** (1867)
from Act Five

CHARACTERS

Button-molder
Peer
Solveig

[*Peer Gynt*, published in 1867, tells the story of its title character in a form reminiscent of a mythological quest — a vast, globe-spanning journey filled with fanciful experiences. But Peer's quest is not to annex new lands, conquer dragons, or find a sacred chalice; he is, instead, in search of something he might claim as a *self*. His adventures take him underground (or, perhaps, into the realm of the subconscious) to the troll kingdom; across the seas to Morocco and Egypt; to heights of wealth and power and depths of madness and despair; and finally, in the following excerpt, back to the patient and loving arms of Solveig, the woman he left behind to find himself. In this ironic echo of the biblical Prodigal Son (not to mention Homer's Odysseus and his faithful Penelope), Ibsen completes Peer's tumultuous, antiheroic circular journey in a gentle key, leaving the audience to wonder whether Peer's quest (and all it stands for) has been in vain. The Button-molder, an enigmatic figure whose literal profession (melting down scraps of metal in a ladle to make buttons) stands metaphorically for a more spiritual kind of recycling, accosts Peer one last time on his way home to Solveig's hut.]

BUTTON-MOLDER: Good morning, Peer Gynt. Where's your record of sins?

PEER: Don't you think I've been whistling and shouting
      For all I'm worth?
BUTTON-MOLDER: And you met no one at all?
PEER: None but a traveling photographer.
BUTTON-MOLDER: So, time has run out.
PEER: Everything's run out.
The owl smells its prey. Can you hear it hooting?
BUTTON-MOLDER: That's the matins bell ringing.
PEER: What is that gleaming?
BUTTON-MOLDER: Only light from a hut.
PEER: And that sound like sighing — ?
BUTTON-MOLDER: Just a woman singing.
PEER: Yes, there! — There's where I'll find
      My record of sins!
BUTTON-MOLDER: (*Seizing hold of him.*) Set your house in order!

(*They have emerged from the wood and are standing near the hut.*)

PEER: Set my house in order? It is there! Leave me!
      Get going! If your ladle were as huge as a coffin,
      I tell you, it's too small for me and my sins.
BUTTON-MOLDER: Until the third crossroad, Peer, but *then* — !

(*Turns aside and goes.*)

PEER: (*Approaching the hut.*) Forward or back, it's just as far.
      Out or in, I'm trapped as before. (*Stops.*)
      No! — Like a wild, unending lament,
      I hear, "Go in, go home, return."

(*Takes a few steps, but stops again.*)

Go round about, said the Bøyg!
(*Hears singing in the hut.*) No! This time,
Straight through, however narrow the path!

(He runs toward the house. At the same moment, Solveig appears in the doorway, dressed for church and with her psalm book wrapped in a kerchief. She has a staff in her hand. She stands upright and gentle.)

PEER: *(Throwing himself down on the threshold.)*

If you're to condemn this sinner, speak out now!

SOLVEIG: He is here! He is here! Praise be to God! *(She gropes for him.)*

PEER: Cry out how sinfully I have offended!

SOLVEIG: You've sinned in nothing, my only boy!

(She gropes again and finds him.)

BUTTON-MOLDER: *(Behind the hut.)* The list, Peer Gynt!

PEER: Cry out my guilt!

SOLVEIG: *(Sitting beside him.)* You've made my life a beautiful song.

Bless you, that you've come home at last.

Blessëd this meeting at Pentecost.

PEER: Then I'm lost!

SOLVEIG: There is one who leads the way.

PEER: Lost, unless you can solve a riddle!

SOLVEIG: Name it.

PEER: Name it? All right — here it is!

Say where's Peer Gynt been since we last met.

SOLVEIG: Been?

PEER: With his destiny's mark upon his brow:

Been since he sprang new from God's thought!

Can you tell me that? If not, I go home —

Below, to the land of mist and shadows.

SOLVEIG: *(Smiling.)* Oh, that riddle's easy.

PEER: Then tell what you know!

Was I ever myself? Where, whole and true?

Myself, with God's seal stamped on my brow?

SOLVEIG: In my faith, in my hope, and in my love.

PEER: *(Stepping back.)* What are you saying? These are riddling words!

The child born in that thought — you are its mother?

SOLVEIG: I am, I am! But who is his father?
>He who forgives when the mother implores.
PEER: (*A ray of light breaks over him and he cries.*)
>My mother; my wife; purest of women! —
>Oh hide me, hide me, within.

>(*He clings to her and hides his face in her lap. Long silence. The sun rises.*)

SOLVEIG: (*Softly singing.*)
>Sleep my dear, my darling boy!
>I will comfort and watch over you —

>The boy has sat on his mother's knee;
>The two have played the lifelong day.

>The boy has slept on his mother's breast
>The lifelong day. God make him blessed.

>The boy has lain near my heart's core
>The lifelong day. He is weary and sore.

>Sleep my dear, my dearest boy!
>I will comfort and watch over you.

BUTTON-MOLDER: (*Behind the hut.*) We'll meet at the next cross-roads, Peer.
>Then we shall see — I'll say no more.
SOLVEIG: (*Singing louder in the increasing daylight.*)
>I will comfort and watch over you;
>Sleep and dream, my dearest boy!

****

from **A Doll House** (1879)
from Act Three

CHARACTERS

Torvald Helmer
Nora Helmer

[*A Doll House* offers one of the most famous endings in Western drama, "the door-slam heard round the world" in Bernard Shaw's inimitable phrase. The sight of a wife and mother leaving her husband and children — and neither returning, penitential, to the nest in the next scene, or suffering the severe punishment of poetic justice via offstage calamity — was without precedent on the European stage. So strongly embedded was this structural and cultural code of behavior that, the story goes, the initial audiences for *A Doll House* in Germany did not realize that the play had ended and sat patiently awaiting what surely must be a final scene of resolution. Ibsen even, against his better judgment, provided such a scene to resolve the aesthetic and thematic dissonance that Nora's unresolved departure created, but then quickly withdrew it, returning to the open-ended, devastating, and still shocking ending as originally written.

There is, however, a moment of almost equally unprecedented force — of paradigm-shifting radicalism — in this last scene, and that is where we will begin our excerpt. It is a quieter moment by far than the door slam, but it has, perhaps, more far-reaching implications for the struggle toward truth, identity, self-knowledge, and personal freedom that would animate so much of the final Prose, or Realist, Cycle, in which *A Doll House* is the second of twelve plays. It is the moment when Nora, emerging from her room having changed out of her tarantella costume and into her street clothes (instead of the nightgown that Torvald expects), resolves to engage, finally, after eight years of marriage (which might stand as a metaphor for centuries of conventional marital relations), in a serious dialogue with her husband. (Translated by Rick Davis and Brian Johnston.)]

HELMER: . . . What's this? You've changed your dress?

NORA: Yes, Torvald, I've changed my dress.

HELMER: But why now, so late?

NORA: I'm not sleeping tonight.

HELMER: But Nora, dear —

NORA: *(Looking at her watch.)* It's not all that late. Sit down, Torvald. We have a great deal to talk about together.

(He sits at one end of the table.)

HELMER: Nora — what's going on? That hard expression —

NORA: Sit down. This will take time. I have a lot to say to you.

HELMER: *(Sits at table directly opposite.)* You're worrying me, Nora. I don't understand you.

NORA: No, that's just it. You don't understand me. And I have never understood you — not until tonight. No — no interruptions. You have to hear me out. We're settling accounts, Torvald.

HELMER: What do you mean by that?

NORA: *(After a short silence.)* Doesn't one thing strike you about the way we're sitting here?

HELMER: What might that be?

NORA: We've been married for eight years. Doesn't it strike you that this is the first time that the two of us — you and I, man and wife — have ever talked seriously?

HELMER: Well — *"seriously"* — what does that mean?

NORA: In eight whole years — no, longer — right from the moment we met, we haven't exchanged one serious word on one serious subject.

HELMER: Should I constantly be involving you in problems you couldn't possibly help me solve?

NORA: I'm not talking about problems. I'm saying that we've never sat down together and seriously tried to get to the bottom of anything.

HELMER: But Nora, dearest — would you have wanted that?

NORA: Yes, of course, that's just it. You've never understood me. A great wrong has been done me, Torvald. First by Papa, then by you.

HELMER: What! By us — who've loved you more than anyone in the world.

NORA: *(Shaking her head.)* You've never loved me. You just thought it was a lot of fun to be in love with me.

HELMER: Nora, how can you say that?

NORA: It's a fact, Torvald. When I was at home with Papa, he told me all his opinions; so of course I had the same opinions. And if I had any others, I kept them hidden, because he wouldn't have liked that. He called me his doll-child, and he played with me like I played with my dolls. Then I came to your house—

HELMER: What kind of way is that to describe our marriage?

NORA: *(Undisturbed.)* I mean, I went from Papa's hands into yours. You set up everything according to your taste; of course I had the same taste, or I pretended to, I'm not really sure. I think it was half-and-half, one as much as the other. Now that I look back on it, I can see that I've lived like a beggar in this house, from hand to mouth; I've lived by doing tricks for you, Torvald. But that's how you wanted it. You and Papa have committed a great sin against me. It's your fault that I've become what I am.

HELMER: Nora — this is unreasonable, and it's ungrateful! Haven't you been happy here?

NORA: No, never. I thought so, but I never really was.

HELMER: Not — not happy!

NORA: No, just having fun. You've always been very nice to me. But our home has never been anything but a playpen. I've been your doll-wife here, just like I was Papa's dollchild at home. And my children, in turn, have been my dolls. It was fun when you came and played with me, just like they had fun when I played with them. That's what our marriage has been, Torvald.

HELMER: There's some truth in this — as exaggerated and hysterical as it is. But from now on, things will be different. Playtime is over: now the teaching begins.

NORA: Who gets this teaching? Me or the children?

HELMER: Both you and the children, my dearest Nora.

NORA: Ah, Torvald: you're not the man to teach me how to be a good wife to you.

HELMER: You can say that!

NORA: And me — how can I possibly teach the children?

HELMER: Nora!

NORA: Didn't you say that yourself, not too long ago? You didn't dare trust them to me?

HELMER: In the heat of the moment! How can you take that seriously?

NORA: Yes, but you spoke the truth. I'm not equal to the task. There's another task I have to get through first. I have try to teach myself. And you can't help me there. I've got to do it alone. And so I'm leaving you.

HELMER: *(Springing up.)* What did you say?

NORA: If I'm going to find out anything about myself — about everything out there — I have to stand completely on my own. That's why I can't stay with you any longer.

HELMER: Nora, Nora!

NORA: I'll leave right away. Kristine can put me up for tonight —

HELMER: You're out of your mind! I won't allow it — I forbid you!

NORA: It's no use forbidding me anything anymore. I'll take what's mine with me. I won't take anything from you, now or later.

HELMER: What kind of madness is this?

NORA: Tomorrow I'm going home — back to my old hometown, I mean. It'll be easier for me to find something to do up there.

HELMER: You blind, inexperienced creature!

NORA: I have to try to get some experience, Torvald.

HELMER: Abandon your home, your husband, your children! Do you have any idea what people will say?

NORA: I can't worry about that. I only know what I have to do.

HELMER: It's grotesque! You're turning your back on your most sacred duties!

NORA: What do you think those are — my most sacred duties?

HELMER: I have to tell you? Aren't they to your husband and children?

NORA: I have other duties, equally sacred.

HELMER: No you don't! Like what?

NORA: Duties to myself.

HELMER: You're a wife and mother, first and foremost.

NORA: I don't believe that anymore. I believe that, first and foremost, I'm a human being — just as much as you — or at least I should try to become one. I'm aware that most people agree with you, Torvald, and that your opinion is backed up by plenty of books. But I can't be satisfied anymore with what most people say, or what's written in the books. Now I've got to think these things through myself, and understand them.

HELMER: What don't you understand about your place in your own home? Don't you have an infallible teacher for questions like this? Don't you have your religion?

NORA: Oh, Torvald, I really don't know what religion is.

HELMER: What are you saying?

NORA: I only know what Pastor Hansen said when I was confirmed. He told me that religion was this and that and the other thing. When I get away from here, when I'm alone, I'll look into that subject too. I'll see if what Pastor Hansen said is true — or at least, if it's true for me.

HELMER: These things just aren't right for a young woman to be saying. If religion can't get through to you, let me try your conscience. You do have some moral feeling? Or — answer me — maybe not?

NORA: Well, Torvald, it's not easy to answer that. I really don't know. I'm actually quite confused about these things. I only know that my ideas are totally different from yours. I find out that the law is not what I thought it was — but I can't get it into my head that the law is right. A woman has no right to spare her dying father's feelings, or save her husband's life! I just can't believe these things.

HELMER: You're talking like a child. You don't understand the society you live in.

NORA: No, I don't. But now I'm going to find out for myself. I've got to figure out who's right — the world or me.

HELMER: You're ill, Nora — you have a fever. I almost think you're out of your mind.

NORA: I've never been so clear — and so certain — about so many things as I am tonight.

HELMER: You're clear and certain that you'll desert your husband and children?

NORA: Yes, I will.

HELMER: There's only one explanation left.

NORA: What is it?

HELMER: You no longer love me.

NORA: No. That's precisely it.

HELMER: Nora! — you can say that!

NORA: Oh, it hurts so much, Torvald. Because you've always been so kind to me. But I can't help it. I don't love you anymore.

HELMER: *(Struggling to control himself.)* Are you also clear and certain about that?

NORA: Yes, absolutely clear and certain. That's why I can't live here anymore.

HELMER: Can you tell me how I lost your love?

NORA: Yes, I can. It was this evening, when the wonderful thing didn't happen — then I saw that you weren't the man I thought you were.

HELMER: Say more — I'm not following this.

NORA: I've waited so patiently for ten years now — good Lord. I know that these wonderful things don't come along every day. Then this disaster broke over me, and I was absolutely certain: now the wonderful thing is coming. While Krogstad's letter was lying out there, I never imagined you'd give in to his terms, even for a minute. I was so certain you'd say to him: tell your story to the whole world! And when that was done —

HELMER: Yes, then what? When I'd given my wife up to shame and disgrace — !

NORA: When that was done, I was completely certain that you would step forward and take everything on yourself — you'd say "I am the guilty one."

HELMER: Nora!

NORA: You're thinking that I'd never accept such a sacrifice from you? No, of course I wouldn't. But what good would my protests be over yours? *That* was the wonderful thing I was hoping for, and in terror of. And to prevent it, I was willing to end my life.

HELMER: I'd work for you night and day, Nora — gladly — suffer and sacrifice for your sake. But no one gives up his honor for the one he loves.

NORA: That's exactly what millions of women have done.

HELMER: Oh — ! You're thinking and talking like an ignorant child.

NORA: Maybe. But you don't think — or talk — like the man I could choose to be with. When your big fright was over — not the danger I was in, but what might happen to you — when that threat was past, then it was like nothing happened to you. I was just what I was before, your little songbird, your doll, and you'd have to take care of it twice as hard as before, since it was so frail and fragile. In that moment, Torvald, it dawned on me that I'd been living with a stranger — that I'd borne three children with him — . Aah — I can't stand the thought of it! I could tear myself to pieces.

HELMER: *(Heavily.)* I see. I see. A gulf has really opened up between us. But Nora, can't we fill it in somehow?

NORA: The way I am now, I'm no wife for you.

HELMER: I can transform myself — I have the strength for it.

NORA: Maybe — if your doll is taken away from you.

HELMER: To live without — without you! Nora, I can't bear the thought of it!

NORA: All the more reason it has to happen.

(Having gone in to the right, she returns with her outdoor clothes and a traveling bag that she sets on a chair by the table.)

HELMER: Nora, Nora, not now! Wait until tomorrow.

NORA: *(Puts on her coat.)* I can't spend the night in a strange man's house.

HELMER: Can't we live here like brother and sister?

NORA: *(Tying her hat.)* You know very well how long that would last. *(Throws her shawl around her.)* Goodbye, Torvald. I won't see the children. They're in better hands than mine, that much I know. The way I am now, I can't do anything for them.

HELMER: But someday, Nora — someday — ?

NORA: How do I know? I have no idea what will become of me.

HELMER: But you're my wife, right now and always, no matter what becomes of you.

NORA: Listen, Torvald; when a wife deserts her husband's house, as I'm doing now, I've heard that the law frees him from any responsibility to her. And anyway, I'm freeing you. From everything. Complete freedom on both sides. See, here's your ring. Give me mine.

HELMER: Even that.

NORA: Even that.

HELMER: Here it is.

NORA: So. Well, now it's finished. I'm putting the keys here. As far as the household goes, the maids know all about it — better than I do. Tomorrow, after I'm gone, Kristine will come and pack the things I brought from home. I'll have them sent.

HELMER: All finished, all over! Nora — will you never think about me after this?

NORA: Of course I'll think about you often — and the children, and the house — .

HELMER: Could I write to you, Nora?

NORA: No, never. You can't do that.

HELMER: But I'll have to send you —

NORA: Nothing; nothing.

HELMER: — help you, if you need —

NORA: No. I'm telling you, I accept nothing from strangers.

HELMER: Nora — can't I ever be anything more than a stranger to you?

NORA: *(Taking her traveling bag.)* Oh Torvald — not unless the most wonderful thing of all were to happen —

HELMER: Name it — what is this most wonderful thing?

NORA: It's — both you and I would have to transform ourselves to the point that — oh, Torvald, I don't know if I believe in it anymore —

HELMER: But I will. Name it! Transform ourselves to the point that —

NORA: That our living together could become a marriage. Goodbye.

(She goes through the hall door.)

HELMER: *(Sinking down into a chair by the door and burying his face in his hands.)* Empty. She's not here. *(A hope flares up in him.)* The most wonderful thing of all — ?

(From below, the sound of a door slamming shut.)

****

from **Ghosts** (1881)
from Act Three

CHARACTERS

Osvald

Mrs. Alving

[*Ghosts* follows *A Doll House* in the cycle and takes up the questions of truth, identity, and freedom in a dialectical relationship with both the earlier play and the following one, *An Enemy of the People*. In *Ghosts*, Mrs. Alving strives to undo an inheritance of deceit — and its material correlative, a personal fortune — that her late husband, Captain Alving, would pass on to their son, Osvald, a painter. She makes sure Osvald goes away to Paris to practice his art, and back home in Norway she uses the Captain's money to build an orphanage, thereby turning it to a good purpose. But Osvald returns home, suffering from a neurological ailment that, his doctor informs him, is inherited and will be incapacitating and ultimately fatal. The orphanage burns to the ground, and the Captain's only physical estate lives on in Osvald's illness. The ending of *Ghosts* presents Mrs. Alving with an impossible choice: to administer the morphine capsules as Osvald has asked her to do in his last extremity, or to hold on to what remains of his life. In this scene, we see Mrs. Alving struggling against the "ghosts" of the ideas, actions, and beliefs of the past that have placed her in that most tragic of human circumstances, where no available choice seems to be the right one. (Translated by Rick Davis and Brian Johnston.)]

OSVALD: (*Muttering to himself.*) It's all insane.

MRS. ALVING: (*Goes over behind him and lays her hands on his shoulders.*) Osvald — my dear boy — all this has given you an awful shock, hasn't it?

OSVALD: (*Turning his face toward her.*) About Father, you mean?

MRS. ALVING: Yes, your unfortunate father. I'm afraid it's been too much for you.

OSVALD: How can you think that? It was a surprise, of course — but finally it can't make much difference to me.

MRS. ALVING: *(Withdrawing her hands.)* No difference — that your father was so incredibly unhappy?

OSVALD: Naturally I'm sympathetic, as I would be for anyone else, but —

MRS. ALVING: And that's all? For your own father.

OSVALD: Oh yes, Father, Father! I never knew anything about my father. All I remember is the time he made me throw up.

MRS. ALVING: That's terrible, to think like that! Shouldn't a child love his father no matter what?

OSVALD: When the child had nothing to thank his father for? Never knew him? You're so enlightened in so many ways — can you really cling to that old superstition?

MRS. ALVING: You say it's only a superstition?

OSVALD: Yes — you see that, Mother, I'm sure. It's just one of those ideas that gets started in the world and then —

MRS. ALVING: *(Shaken.)* Ghosts!

OSVALD: *(Walks across the floor.)* Yes, you certainly could call them ghosts.

MRS. ALVING: *(Crying out.)* Osvald — then you don't love me either!

OSVALD: But at least I know you.

MRS. ALVING: Yes — but that's all?

OSVALD: And I know how much you care for me and I'm very grateful for that. You can be enormously useful to me now that I'm sick.

MRS. ALVING: Yes, I can, Osvald, can't I! I could almost bless this illness that drove you home to me. Because now I can see it: I don't have you yet, I'll have to win you.

OSVALD: *(Impatiently.)* Yes, yes, yes. This is all just talk. Remember I'm a sick man, Mother. I can't worry about others; I have enough to do just thinking about myself.

MRS. ALVING: *(Softly.)* I'll be patient and calm.

OSVALD: And cheerful, Mother!

MRS. ALVING: Yes, my dear, dear boy, you're right. *(Goes over to him.)* Now have I taken away all your remorse? No more reproaching yourself?

OSVALD: Yes, you have. But who will take away the dread?

MRS. ALVING: Dread?

OSVALD: *(Walks across the room.)* Regina would have done it at a word from me.

MRS. ALVING: I don't understand. What's this about dread — and Regina?

OSVALD: Is it late, Mother?

MRS. ALVING: Early morning. *(Looking out through the garden room.)* Up in the mountains the day is beginning to break. And it's going to be a clear day, Osvald! In a little while you'll get to see the sun.

OSVALD: That'll be a joy. Oh, there can be so much to live for —

MRS. ALVING: Yes, I know!

OSVALD: And even if I can't work —

MRS. ALVING: Oh, you'll be able to work again soon. Now that you don't have to brood about these depressing ideas any more.

OSVALD: No, that's true. It's good that you could knock down all those delusions of mine. And when I get rid of this one last thing — *(Sits on the sofa.)* Now, Mother, we've got to have a talk.

MRS. ALVING: All right. *(She pushes an armchair over to the sofa and sits beside him.)*

OSVALD: And then the sun will rise. And then you'll know. And then I'll no longer have this dread.

MRS. ALVING: What will I know? Tell me.

OSVALD: *(Not listening to her.)* Mother, didn't you say that you'd do anything for me, anything in the world, if I asked you?

MRS. ALVING: That's what I said.

OSVALD: Do you stand by that?

MRS. ALVING: You can depend on it, my only boy. You're what I live for now, nothing else.

OSVALD: All right. Now you'll hear it. Mother, you have a strong mind, I know you can take this in — so now you must sit calmly while you hear what it is.

MRS. ALVING: What could be so horrible?

OSVALD: And don't scream. You hear me? Promise me that? We'll sit and talk about it quietly. Promise me that, Mother?

MRS. ALVING: Yes, yes. I promise — just tell me!

OSVALD: Well, all this talk about my being tired — about not being able to think about work — that isn't the illness, only the symptoms.

MRS. ALVING: What is the illness?

OSVALD: The illness I received as my inheritance — *(Points to his forehead.)* It sits right here.

MRS. ALVING: *(Almost speechless.)* Osvald! No, no!

OSVALD: Don't scream. I can't stand it. Yes, Mother, it sits right here, lurking, ready to break out any day, any time.

MRS. ALVING: Horrible!

OSVALD: Just be calm. That's how it is with me.

MRS. ALVING: *(Jumping up.)* It's not true, Osvald! It's impossible! It can't be!

OSVALD: I had one attack down there, it didn't last long. But when I found out what had happened to me, this dread began pursuing me, relentlessly, and so I started back home to you as fast as I could.

MRS. ALVING: And that's the dread — !

OSVALD: Yes, it's revolting beyond words. Don't you see that? Some plain old terminal disease I could — I'm not afraid of dying, even though I'd like to live as long as I can.

MRS. ALVING: Yes, Osvald — you've got to!

OSVALD: But this is beyond disgusting. To be turned into a helpless child again — to have to be fed, to have to be — it's unspeakable!

MRS. ALVING: My child has his mother to take care of him.

OSVALD: *(Leaps up.)* Never, that's exactly what I don't want. I can't stand the idea of lying there for years like that, turning old and gray. And meanwhile you might die before me. *(Sits in Mrs. Alving's chair.)* The doctor said it wouldn't necessarily be fatal right away. He called it a kind of softening of the brain, or something like that.

(Smiles sadly.) I think that sounds so charming — it always makes me think of red velvet curtains — something soft and delicate to stroke.

MRS. ALVING: *(Screaming.)* Osvald!

OSVALD: *(Leaps up again and walks across the room.)* And now you've taken Regina away from me! If only I had her. She'd have given me a helping hand, yes she would.

MRS. ALVING: *(Goes over to him.)* What do you mean, my boy? What help is there in the world that I wouldn't give you?

OSVALD: When I'd recovered from my attack down there, the doctor told me that when it came again — and it will come again — that then it'd be beyond hope.

MRS. ALVING: He was heartless enough to —

OSVALD: I demanded it. I told him I had plans to make — *(Smiles slyly.)* And so I had. *(Takes a little box from his inside breast pocket.)* See this, Mother?

MRS. ALVING: What is it?

OSVALD: Morphine powder.

MRS. ALVING: *(Looks at him in horror.)* Osvald — my boy!

OSVALD: I've managed to save twelve capsules.

MRS. ALVING: *(Grabbing for it.)* Give me the box, Osvald!

OSVALD: Not yet, Mother! *(He puts it back in his pocket.)*

MRS. ALVING: I can't live through this!

OSVALD: You have to live through it. If Regina were here I'd have told her how things are, and begged her for this last bit of help. And she would have helped me, I'm sure of it.

MRS. ALVING: Never!

OSVALD: When the horrible thing happened, and she saw me lying there like an imbecile, like a child, helpless, lost, beyond hope of rescue —

MRS. ALVING: Regina would never have done that!

OSVALD: Regina would have done it! She was so splendid, so light-hearted, she would have gotten tired pretty fast of looking after an invalid like me.

MRS. ALVING: Well then. Give thanks that Regina's not here!

OSVALD: So — now you have to give me that helping hand, Mother.

MRS. ALVING: (*With a loud scream.*) I!

OSVALD: Who else? Who's closer?

MRS. ALVING: I! Your Mother!

OSVALD: Exactly why.

MRS. ALVING: I, who gave you life!

OSVALD: I didn't ask you for life. And what kind of life have you given me? I don't want it. Take it back!

MRS. ALVING: Help, help! (*She runs into the hall.*)

OSVALD: (*Pursuing her.*) Don't leave me! Where are you going?

MRS. ALVING: (*In the hall.*) To get the doctor, Osvald! Let me go!

OSVALD: (*In the hall.*) You're not leaving. And no one's coming in. (*A key is turned in a lock.*)

MRS. ALVING: (*Coming in again.*) Osvald! Osvald! — my child!

OSVALD: (*Following her.*) Where's your Mother's heart? Can you stand to see me suffer this unspeakable dread?

MRS. ALVING: (*After a moment's silence, says firmly.*) Here's my hand on it.

OSVALD: Will you — ?

MRS. ALVING: If necessary. But it won't be necessary. No, never — it's not possible!

OSVALD: Well, let's hope so. And let's live together as long as we can. Thank you, Mother.

(*He sits in the armchair that Mrs. Alving had moved over to the sofa. The day is breaking. The lamp is still burning on the table.*)

MRS. ALVING: (*Approaching him cautiously.*) Do you feel more at peace now?

OSVALD: Yes.

MRS. ALVING: (*Bends over him.*) You've been carrying a terrible delusion inside, Osvald — but it was all a delusion. Of course you couldn't bear all these agonies. But now you'll get your rest, here at home with your mother, my blessed boy. Anything you want, anything you point out to me, you'll have it! Just like when you were a little child. See, there. The sickness is gone — see how easily it went away! I knew it would. And look, Osvald, what a beautiful day we're going to have. Brilliant sunshine. Now you can really see your home.

(She goes over to the table and puts out the lamp. Sunrise. The glaciers and peaks in the background lie in brilliant morning light.)

OSVALD: *(Sits in the armchair with his back to this view, without stirring. Suddenly he says.)* Mother, give me the sun.

MRS. ALVING: *(By the table, looks at him, startled.)* What did you say?

OSVALD: *(Repeats dully and tonelessly.)* The sun. The sun.

MRS. ALVING: *(Goes over to him.)* Osvald, what's the matter with you?

(Osvald seems to shrink in the chair. All the muscles loosen. His face is expressionless. His eyes stare vacantly.)

MRS. ALVING: *(Shaking in terror.)* What is this? *(Screams loudly.)* Osvald! What's the matter with you! *(Throws herself down on her knees beside him and shakes him.)* Osvald! Osvald! Look at me! Don't you know me!

OSVALD: *(Tonelessly, as before.)* The sun. The sun.

MRS. ALVING: *(Springs up in anguish. Tears at her hair with both hands and screams.)* This is unbearable! *(Whispers as though terrified.)* Unbearable! Never! *(Suddenly.)* Where did he put them? *(Fumbling hastily in his pocket.)* Here! *(Retreats a few steps and screams.)* No, no, no! — Yes! No, no!

(She stands a few steps from him, her hands clutching her hair, staring at him in speechless horror.)

OSVALD: *(Sits motionless as before, and says.)* The sun. The sun.

****

from **Hedda Gabler** (1890)
from Act Four

CHARACTERS

Hedda
Brack
Tesman
Mrs. Elvsted

[On a deceptively domestic stage and an apparently middle-class, human scale, *Hedda Gabler* sets up a war of the worlds between the ancient, anarchic, yet hugely creative forces of paganism and the centuries of Christian practices that seek to contain them, substituting order for chaos, spirit for flesh, and (in the world of the play) routine for improvisation, whether intellectual, emotional, or spiritual. Hedda and Eilert Løvborg (he of the Dionysian "vine leaves in his hair") and to a certain extent Judge Brack, whose libido at least is Dionysian even if his public persona is safely conventional, seek to upset the order that Hedda's new husband, George Tesman, would seek to impose on everything from his pedestrian historical scholarship to their home and married life. Just before the scene presented here, we learn that Løvborg has shot himself. At first, Hedda tries to interpret it as an act of liberation, of beauty; but the Judge directs her toward a less heroic view of the episode. Meanwhile, Tesman and Thea, a friend of Løvborg's who has been helping him with his own (quite brilliant) scholarship, conceive the idea of putting his notes together into a work that would stand as a memorial to him. From there, the play takes several quick and unexpected turns in both tonality and plot. The ending is one of the most sudden, definitive, yet ambiguous in all of drama, even prompting some critics to see a note of dark comedy in the moments leading up to the climactic action and the brief, incredulous response just before the final curtain. (Translated by Rick Davis and Brian Johnston.)]

HEDDA: *(Softly.)* Ah, Judge — This act of Eilert Løvborg's — There's a sense of liberation in it.

BRACK: Liberation, Mrs. Hedda? Yes, I guess it's a liberation for him all right.

HEDDA: I mean, for me. It's a liberation for me to know that in this world an act of such courage, done in full, free will is possible. Something bathed in a bright shaft of sudden beauty.

BRACK: *(Smiles.)* Hmm — Dear Mrs. Hedda —

HEDDA: Oh, I know what you're going to say because you're a kind of specialist too, after all, just like — Ah well.

BRACK: *(Looking steadily at her.)* Eilert Løvborg meant more to you than you might admit — even to yourself. Or am I wrong?

HEDDA: I don't answer questions like that. All I know is that Eilert Løvborg had the courage to live life his own way, and now — his last great act — bathed in beauty. He — had the will to break away from the banquet of life — so soon.

BRACK: It pains me, Mrs. Hedda — but I'm forced to shatter this pretty illusion of yours.

HEDDA: Illusion?

BRACK: Which would have been taken away from you soon enough.

HEDDA: And what's that?

BRACK: He didn't shoot himself — so freely.

HEDDA: Not freely?

BRACK: No. This whole Eilert Løvborg business didn't come off exactly the way I described it.

HEDDA: *(In suspense.)* Are you hiding something? What is it?

BRACK: I employed a few euphemisms for poor Mrs. Elvsted's sake.

HEDDA: Such as — ?

BRACK: First, of course, he's already dead.

HEDDA: At the hospital?

BRACK: Yes. And without regaining consciousness.

HEDDA: What else?

BRACK: The incident took place somewhere other than his room.

HEDDA: That's insignificant.

BRACK: Not completely. I have to tell you — Eilert Løvborg was found shot in — Miss Diana's boudoir.

HEDDA: (*About to jump up but sinks back again.*) That's impossible, Judge. He can't have gone there again today.

BRACK: He was there this afternoon. He came to demand the return of something that he said they'd taken from him. He talked crazily about a lost child.

HEDDA: Ah, so that's why —

BRACK: I thought maybe he was referring to his manuscript but I hear he'd already destroyed that himself so I guess it was his pocketbook.

HEDDA: Possibly. So — that's where he was found.

BRACK: Right there with a discharged pistol in his coat pocket, and a fatal bullet wound.

HEDDA: In the chest, yes?

BRACK: No — lower down.

HEDDA: (*Looks up at him with an expression of revulsion.*) That too! Oh absurdity — ! It hangs like a curse over everything I so much as touch.

BRACK: There's still one more thing, Mrs. Hedda. Also in the ugly category.

HEDDA: And what is that?

BRACK: The pistol he had with him—

HEDDA: (*Breathless.*) Well, what about it?

BRACK: He must have stolen it.

HEDDA: (*Jumping up.*) Stolen? That's not true. He didn't.

BRACK: There's no other explanation possible. He must have stolen it — Shh.

(*Tesman and Mrs. Elvsted have gotten up from the table in the rear room and come into the living room.*)

TESMAN: *(With papers in both hands.)* Hedda, my dear — I can hardly see anything in there under that lamp. Just think —

HEDDA: I'm thinking.

TESMAN: Do you think you might let us sit a while at your desk, hm?

HEDDA: Oh, gladly. *(Quickly.)* No, wait. Let me just clean it up a bit first.

TESMAN: Oh, not necessary, Hedda. There's plenty of room.

HEDDA: No, no, I'll just straighten it up, I'm telling you. I'll just move these things here under the piano for a while.

(She has pulled an object covered with sheet music out of the bookcase. She adds a few more sheets and carries the whole pile out to the left of the rear room. Tesman puts the papers on the desk and brings over the lamp from the corner table. He and Mrs. Elvsted sit and continue the work.)

HEDDA: Well, Thea, my sweet. Are things moving along with the memorial?

MRS. ELVSTED: *(Looks up at her dejectedly.)* Oh, God — It's going to be so difficult to find the order in all of this.

TESMAN: But it must be done. There's simply no other choice. And finding the order in other people's papers — that's precisely what I'm meant for.

(Hedda goes over to the stove and sits on one of the stools. Brack stands over her, leaning over the armchair.)

HEDDA: *(Whispers.)* What were you saying about the pistol?

BRACK: *(Softly.)* That he must have stolen it.

HEDDA: Why stolen exactly?

BRACK: Because there shouldn't be any other way to explain it, Mrs. Hedda.

HEDDA: I see.

BRACK: *(Looks briefly at her.)* Eilert Løvborg was here this morning, am I correct?

HEDDA: Yes.

BRACK: Were you alone with him?

HEDDA: Yes, for a while.

BRACK: You didn't leave the room at all while he was here?

HEDDA: No.

BRACK: Think again. Weren't you out of the room, even for one moment?

HEDDA: Yes. Perhaps. Just for a moment — out in the hallway.

BRACK: And where was your pistol case at that time?

HEDDA: I put it under the —

BRACK: Well, Mrs. Hedda —

HEDDA: It was over there on the writing table.

BRACK: Have you looked since then to see if both pistols are there?

HEDDA: No.

BRACK: It's not necessary. I saw the pistol Løvborg had, and recognized it immediately from yesterday, and from before, as well.

HEDDA: Have you got it?

BRACK: No, the police have it.

HEDDA: What will the police do with that pistol?

BRACK: Try to track down its owner.

HEDDA: Do you think they can do that?

BRACK: *(Bends over her and whispers.)* No, Hedda Gabler, not as long as I keep quiet.

HEDDA: *(Looking fearfully at him.)* And what if you don't keep quiet — then what?

BRACK: Then the way out is to claim that the pistol was stolen.

HEDDA: I'd rather die.

BRACK: *(Smiling.)* People make those threats but they don't act on them.

HEDDA: *(Without answering.)* So — let's say the pistol is not stolen and the owner is found out? What happens then?

BRACK: Well, Hedda — then there'll be a scandal.

HEDDA: A scandal?

BRACK: Oh, yes, a scandal. Just what you're so desperately afraid of.

You'd have to appear in court, naturally. You and Miss Diana. She'd have to detail how it all occurred. Whether it was an accident or a homicide. Was he trying to draw the pistol to threaten her? Is that when the gun went off? Did she snatch it out of his hands to shoot him, then put the pistol back in his pocket? That would be thoroughly in character for her. She's a feisty little thing, that Miss Diana.

HEDDA: But all this ugliness has got nothing to do with me.

BRACK: No. But you would have to answer one question. Why did you give the pistol to Eilert Løvborg? And what conclusions would people draw from the fact that you gave it to him?

HEDDA: *(Lowers her head.)* That's true. I didn't think of that.

BRACK: Well. Fortunately you have nothing to worry about as long as I keep quiet.

HEDDA: *(Looking up at him.)* So I'm in your power now, Judge. You have a hold over me from now on.

BRACK: *(Whispering more softly.)* Dearest Hedda — believe me — I won't abuse my position.

HEDDA: But in your power. Totally subject to your demands — And your will. Not free, not free at all. *(She gets up silently.)* No, that's one thought I just can't stand. Never!

BRACK: *(Looks mockingly at her.)* One can usually learn to live with the inevitable.

HEDDA: *(Returning his look.)* Maybe so. *(She goes over to the writing table, suppressing an involuntary smile and imitating Tesman's intonation.)* Well, George, this is going to work out, hm?

TESMAN: Oh, Lord knows, dear. Anyway, at this rate, it's going to be months of work.

HEDDA: *(As before.)* No, just think. *(Runs her fingers lightly through Mrs. Elvsted's hair.)* Doesn't it seem strange, Thea. Here you are, sitting together with Tesman — just like you used to sit with Eilert Løvborg.

MRS. ELVSTED: Oh, God, if only I could inspire your husband too.

HEDDA: Oh, that will come — in time.

TESMAN: Yes, you know what, Hedda — I really think I'm beginning to feel something like that. But why don't you go over and sit with Judge Brack some more.

HEDDA: Can't you two find any use for me here?

TESMAN: No, nothing in the world. (*Turning his head.*) From now on, my dear Judge, you'll have to be kind enough to keep Hedda company.

BRACK: (*With a glance at Hedda.*) That will be an infinite pleasure for me.

HEDDA: Thanks, but I'm tired tonight. I'll go in there and lie down on the sofa for a while.

TESMAN: Yes, do that, Hedda, hm?

(*Hedda goes into the rear room and draws the curtains after her. Short pause. Suddenly she is heard to play a wild dance melody on the piano.*)

MRS. ELVSTED: (*Jumping up from her chair.*) Oh — what's that?

TESMAN: (*Running to the doorway.*) Oh, Hedda, my dear — Don't play dance music tonight. Just think of poor Aunt Rina and of Eilert Løvborg too.

HEDDA: (*Putting her head out from between the curtains.*) And Aunt Julie and all the rest of them too. From now on I shall be quiet. (*She closes the curtains again.*)

TESMAN: (*At the writing table.*) This can't be making her very happy — Seeing us at this melancholy work. You know what, Mrs. Elvsted — You're going to move in with Aunt Julie. Then I can come over in the evening, and we can sit and work there, hm?

MRS. ELVSTED: Yes, maybe that would be the best —

HEDDA: (*From the rear room.*) I can hear you perfectly well, Tesman. So, how am I supposed to get through the evenings out here?

TESMAN: (*Leafing through the papers.*) Oh, I'm sure Judge Brack will be good enough to call on you.

BRACK: (*In the armchair, shouts merrily.*) I'd be delighted, Mrs. Tesman.

Every evening. Oh, we're going to have some good times together, the two of us.

HEDDA: *(Loudly and clearly.)* Yes, that's what you're hoping for isn't it, Judge? You, the one and only cock of the walk —

(A shot is heard within. Tesman, Mrs. Elvsted and Brack jump to their feet.)

TESMAN: Oh, she's playing around with those pistols again.

(He pulls the curtains aside and runs in. Mrs. Elvsted follows. Hedda is stretched out lifeless on the sofa. Confusion and cries. Berta comes running in from the right.)

TESMAN: *(Shrieking to Brack.)* Shot herself! Shot herself in the temple! Just think!

BRACK : *(Half prostrate in the armchair.)* But God have mercy — People don't act that way.

****

from **The Master Builder** (1892)
from Act Three

CHARACTERS

Solness
Hilda
Mrs. Solness
Ragnar
Dr. Herdal
The Ladies

[Published in 1892, after Ibsen's return to Norway from his years of self-imposed exile, *The Master Builder* begins the final phase of Ibsen's twelve-play Prose, or Realist, Cycle. The world of the play is haunted by domestic tragedy in the past lives of Master Builder Solness and his wife, Aline. At the same time it is suffused with the radical energy of youth "knocking at the door," promising change and danger, especially in the person of Hilda Wangel, a young woman whom Solness met ten years before the action of the play, when she was "twelve — thirteen," and who has returned ostensibly to collect on Solness's fanciful promise to carry her off, after ten years, to the "kingdom of Orangia." As the play drives to its conclusion, the town is gathering for a celebration of Solness's latest building project, a magnificent new home for himself and his wife. In his younger days, Solness would climb to the top of the highest steeples and towers to lay a ceremonial wreath on his finished constructions, but he has given up that practice. Today, however, under Hilda's spell, Solness ponders a new flight to a different kingdom of freedom and happiness and decides once again to climb the tower of his newest creation. (Translated by Brian Johnston.)]

SOLNESS: I hear there's something someone wants me for.
HILDA: Yes, it's me, master builder.

SOLNESS: Ah, then it's you, Hilda. I was afraid it would be Aline or the doctor.

HILDA: There's a lot you're afraid of, isn't there?

SOLNESS: That's what you think?

HILDA: Yes. People say that you're afraid of clambering about — like up on scaffolding.

SOLNESS: Well, that's something all to itself.

HILDA: But you're afraid of it — isn't that true?

SOLNESS: Yes, I am.

HILDA: Afraid of falling and killing yourself?

SOLNESS: No, not of that.

HILDA: Of what, then?

SOLNESS: I'm afraid of retribution, Hilda.

HILDA: Of retribution? *(Shaking her head.)* I don't understand.

SOLNESS: Sit down and I'll tell you something.

HILDA: Yes, do! Right away! *(She sits on a stool by the railing and looks expectantly at him.)*

SOLNESS: *(Throws his hat on the table.)* You know that at first I started out by building churches.

HILDA: *(Nods.)* Yes, I know that all right.

SOLNESS: Because, you see, as a boy I came from a pious home in the country. Therefore I believed that building churches was the noblest vocation I could choose.

HILDA: Yes, yes.

SOLNESS: And I think I dare say I built those poor little country churches with such an ardent and honest spirit that — that —

HILDA: That — ? Yes — ?

SOLNESS: Well, that I believed He should have been pleased with me.

HILDA: He? Which "He?"

SOLNESS: He who was to have the churches. He whom they would serve in honor and glory.

HILDA: I see. But are you so sure that — that He wasn't — pleased with you?

SOLNESS: (Scornfully.) Pleased with me! How can you talk like that, Hilda? He who gave the troll in me permission to run riot as much as it wished. He who summoned them to the spot to serve me day and night — all these — these —

HILDA: Devils —

SOLNESS: Yes, both the one kind and the other. Oh no, I felt sure enough He wasn't pleased with me. (Secretively.) Actually, you see, that was why He let the old house burn down.

HILDA: That was why?

SOLNESS: Yes, don't you see? He wanted me to have the chance to be a master in my own realm — and build even greater churches to His glory. At first I didn't understand what He wanted. But then, all at once, it was clear to me.

HILDA: When was that?

SOLNESS: It was when I built the church tower up at Lysanger.

HILDA: That's what I thought.

SOLNESS: Because you see, Hilda, up in that place where I was a stranger, I used to go around brooding and pondering to myself. And then I saw so clearly why He had taken my small children away from me. It was to make sure nothing else should occupy me. Nothing, like love or happiness, you understand. I was to be a master builder only. Nothing else. And so throughout my whole life I was to go on building for Him. (Laughing.) But that's not how it turned out.

HILDA: What did you do, then?

SOLNESS: First I searched into and tested myself —

HILDA: And then — ?

SOLNESS: Then I did the impossible. I, just like Him.

HILDA: The impossible!

SOLNESS: I'd never before been able to climb high up — high and free. But that day I could.

HILDA: (Jumping up.) Yes, yes, you could!

SOLNESS: And when I stood right up there and hung the wreath over the weathervane, then I said to Him: Hear me, Almighty One!

From this day on I, too, will be a free master builder. In my own realm. Just like you. I will never more build churches for you. Only homes for human beings.

HILDA: *(With large sparkling eyes.)* That was the singing I heard in the air.

SOLNESS: But He still got what He needed for His mill to grind.

HILDA: What do you mean by that?

SOLNESS: *(Looking dejectedly at her.)* This building homes for human beings — it's not worth a penny, Hilda.

HILDA: You say that now?

SOLNESS: Yes, because now I can see that human beings have no use for these homes of theirs. Not for being happy in. And I wouldn't have had use for such a home, either — if I'd owned one. *(With a quiet, bitter laugh.)* So, that's the sum total as far, as far back as I can see. Actually, nothing really built. And nothing sacrificed to be able to build, either. Nothing, nothing, all told.

HILDA: Then you will never build anything new from now on?

SOLNESS: *(Lively.)* Yes, now I'm going to begin.

HILDA: What, then? What, then? Say it straight out!

SOLNESS: The only thing I believe can create human happiness — that's what I'll build, now.

HILDA: *(Looking intently at him.)* Master builder, you mean our castles in the air.

SOLNESS: Yes, castles in the air.

HILDA: I'm afraid you'll get dizzy before we get halfway up.

SOLNESS: Not if I go hand in hand with you, Hilda.

HILDA: *(With a shade of suppressed resentment.)* Only with me? Won't we have others with us?

SOLNESS: What others do you mean?

HILDA: Well, her — that Kaja at the desk. Poor thing, don't you want her along, too?

SOLNESS: Ah, so it was her that Aline sat here talking to you about.

HILDA: Well, is it true or not?

SOLNESS: *(Vehemently.)* I don't answer questions like that! You must trust me totally and entirely.

HILDA: For ten years I've trusted you so completely.

SOLNESS: You must keep on trusting me.

HILDA: Then let me see you up there — high and free!

SOLNESS: *(Heavily.)* Oh, Hilda, I can't do that every day.

HILDA: *(Passionately.)* I will see it! I will see it! *(Begging.)* Just once more, master builder. Do the impossible again!

SOLNESS: *(Looking deeply at her.)* If I did attempt it, Hilda, I'd stand up there and talk to Him as I did last time.

HILDA: *(With mounting excitement.)* What will you say to Him?

SOLNESS: I will say: Hear me, Almighty One — you must now judge me as you see fit. But from now on I will build only the most beautiful thing in the world —

HILDA: *(Enraptured.)* Yes — yes — yes.

SOLNESS: — Build it together with a princess that I love —

HILDA: Yes, tell Him that! Tell Him that!

SOLNESS: Yes. And then I'll say to Him: now I'm going down to hold her in my arms and kiss her —

HILDA: Many times! Say that!

SOLNESS: Many, many times, I'll tell Him.

HILDA: And then — ?

SOLNESS: Then I'll swing my hat — and come down to earth — and do as I said.

HILDA: *(With outstretched arms.)* Now I see you again as if there was singing in the air!

SOLNESS: *(Looking at her with bowed head.)* How did you become what you are, Hilda?

HILDA: How did you make me become what I am?

SOLNESS: *(Brief and curt.)* The princess shall have her castle.

HILDA: *(Jubilant, clapping her hands.)* Oh, master builder! My lovely, lovely castle. Our castle in the air.

SOLNESS: On a solid foundation.

(Out in the street many people have gathered and can be glimpsed fleetingly through the trees. Music from a brass band is heard from behind the new house. Mrs. Solness, with a fur stole round her neck, Dr. Herdal, with her white shawl over his arm, and several ladies come onto the veranda. Ragnar Brovik at the same time approaches from the garden.)

MRS. SOLNESS: *(To Ragnar.)* Is there going to be music, too?

RAGNAR: Yes. It's the Builders Association. *(To Solness.)* The foreman asked me to tell you he's ready now to go up with the wreath.

SOLNESS: *(Taking his hat.)* Good. I'll go down there myself.

MRS. SOLNESS: *(Anxiously.)* What will you be doing down there, Halvard?

SOLNESS: *(Curtly.)* I have to be down there with the men.

MRS. SOLNESS: Yes, down below. Only down below.

SOLNESS: It's what I usually do every time.

MRS. SOLNESS: *(Calling after him from the railing.)* But please tell the man to be careful as he climbs up. Promise me that, Halvard!

DR. HERDAL: *(To Mrs. Solness.)* You see, I was right. He's not thinking anymore about that crazy business.

MRS. SOLNESS: Oh, what a relief. Twice we've had men fall there, and both times they were killed. *(Turning to Hilda.)* Thank you, Miss Wangel, for taking hold of him like that. I know I couldn't have managed it.

DR. HERDAL: *(Merrily.)* Yes, yes, Miss Wangel, you really know how to hold fast to a man when you want to!

(Mrs. Solness and Dr. Herdal go over to the Ladies, who stand near the steps. Hilda remains standing at the railing. Ragnar goes over to her.)

RAGNAR: *(With suppressed laughter, speaking quietly.)* Miss Wangel, do you see all the young people down there in the street?

HILDA: Yes.

RAGNAR: They're my fellow students come to watch the master.

HILDA: What will they be watching for?

RAGNAR: They will watch him not dare to climb to the top of his own house.

HILDA: Is that what the boys will be doing?

RAGNAR: (*Harshly and scornfully.*) He's kept us down for so long. Now we'll be looking as he obligingly keeps himself down.

HILDA: You'll not get to see that. Not today.

RAGNAR: (*Smiling.*) So? How will we get to see him, then?

HILDA: High — high up by the weathervane, that's where you'll see him.

RAGNAR: (*Laughing.*) Him? You want me to believe that!

HILDA: He intends to climb to the top — that's where you'll see him.

RAGNAR: He *intends* to, yes — that I can believe. But he simply won't be able to. He'd be dizzy long, long before he got halfway up. He would have to crawl back down again on hands and knees.

DR. HERDAL: (*Pointing.*) Look! There goes the foreman up the ladder.

MRS. SOLNESS: And he's got to carry the wreath too. Oh, if only he'll be careful.

RAGNAR: (*Crying out in surprise.*) But surely that's —

HILDA: (*In an outburst of joy.*) It's the master builder himself!

MRS. SOLNESS: (*Shrieking in terror.*) Yes, it's Halvard. Oh, dear God! Halvard! Halvard!

DR. HERDAL: Hush. Don't call out to him.

MRS. SOLNESS: (*Half distracted.*) I must go to him! Get him to come down again!

DR. HERDAL: (*Holding onto her.*) Don't anyone move. Not a sound!

HILDA: (*Not moving, following Solness with her eyes.*) He's climbing and climbing. Always higher. Always higher. Look! Just look!

RAGNAR: (*Breathless.*) Now he has to turn back. He can't do anything else!

HILDA: Climbing and climbing. He's nearly there.

MRS. SOLNESS: Oh, I'll die of fright. I can't bear to watch him.

DR. HERDAL: Then don't look at him.

HILDA: He's standing now on the highest plank. Right to the top!

DR. HERDAL: Nobody say anything! You hear me!

HILDA: *(With jubilant, quiet intensity.)* At last! At last! Now I see him great and free again!

RAGNAR: *(Almost speechless.)* But all this is —

HILDA: This is how I've seen him all these ten years. How strong he stands! Fearfully thrilling, after all. Look at him! Now he's hanging the wreath on the spire!

RAGNAR: All this I'm seeing here is completely impossible.

HILDA: Yes, it's the impossible now that he's doing. *(With the inscrutable look in her eyes.)* Can you see anyone else up there with him?

RAGNAR: There's no one else.

HILDA: Yes, there's someone he's struggling with.

RAGNAR: You're mistaken.

HILDA: Can't you hear singing in the air, either?

RAGNAR: It must be the wind in the treetops.

HILDA: I hear a singing. A powerful singing. *(Crying out in joyful exultation.)* Look, look! Now he's waving his hat. Waving to us down here. Oh, wave back up to him there. For now, now it is fulfilled! *(Snatches the white shawl from the doctor, waves it, and cries out.)* Hurray for master builder Solness!

DR. HERDAL: Stop! Stop! For God's sake!

(The Ladies on the veranda wave their handkerchiefs, and shouts of "Hurray" come from the street. Suddenly they stop and the crowd gives out a cry of horror. A human body, along with some planks and branches can be glimpsed falling between the trees.)

MRS. SOLNESS AND THE LADIES: *(At the same time.)* He's falling! He's falling!

(Mrs. Solness sways and sinks back fainting; the Ladies catch her amid cries and confusion. The crowd in the street breaks down the fence and storms into the garden. Dr. Herdal also rushes down below. A short pause.)

HILDA: *(Staring fixedly upward and speaking as if petrified.)* My master builder.

RAGNAR: *(Leans, trembling, against the railing.)* He must be crushed to bits. Killed on the spot.

ONE OF THE LADIES: *(As Mrs. Solness is carried into the house.)* Run down to the doctor —

RAGNAR: I can't move a foot.

ANOTHER LADY: Call down to somebody, then!

RAGNAR: *(Trying to call.)* How is he? Is he alive?

A VOICE: *(In the garden.)* Master builder Solness is dead.

OTHER VOICES: His whole head is crushed. He fell right into the quarry.

HILDA: *(Turning to Ragnar and speaking quietly.)* I can no longer see him up there.

RAGNAR: How horrible this is. So he couldn't do it, after all.

HILDA: *(As if in quiet, subdued triumph.)* But he went right to the top. And I heard harps in the air. *(Swings the shawl up overhead and cries out with wild intensity.)* My — my master builder!

****

from **When We Dead Awaken** (1899)
from Act Three

CHARACTERS

Rubek
Maja
Ulfhejm
Irene
The Nun

[The final play of Ibsen's career (1899) completes the Prose, or Realist, Cycle and, in Ibsen's words, "makes of it an entity." In this dramatic epilogue, a great but creatively stifled sculptor, Rubek, and his wife, Maja, have come to a mountain spa. Rubek encounters his former model and muse, Irene, subject of his masterpiece, *Resurrection Day*, accompanied by a mysterious Nun. Through the figures of the sculptor and the model, Ibsen continues his exploration (so powerful in *The Master Builder*) of the sources of artistic creation and the toll it can take on both artist and subject. Meanwhile, Maja, whose earth-spirit qualities have found little resonance in the rarefied world her husband inhabits, has become friendly with Ulfhejm, a wealthy hunter known as the Bear-Killer. They set off on a hunting expedition, leaving Rubek and Irene to arrange their own mountain rendezvous.

In the excerpt that follows, the couples encounter each other near the mountain peak as a storm begins to build. The avalanche that ends the play, like that of the much earlier *Brand* (1866), is punctuated by a Latin benediction. In *Brand*, an unseen voice sounds the phrase "He is Deus Caritatis" (the God of love); here, the Nun intones the blessing "Pax vobiscum" (Peace be with you), as the snow sweeps Rubek and Irene away, while Maja is heard singing an exultant song of newfound freedom farther down the mountain. (Translated by Brian Johnston.)]

RUBEK: *(Still only half visible over the ridge.)* What — Maja! Are we fated to meet yet again?

MAJA: *(With feigned assurance.)* At your service. Do come on up.

(Rubek climbs up completely and reaches his hand to Irene, who also climbs fully into view.)

RUBEK: *(Coldly to Maja.)* You've also been on the mountain all night, have you? Like us?

MAJA: I've been out hunting, yes. You did give me leave to go.

ULFHEJM: *(Pointing toward the chasm.)* Did you come up the path there?

RUBEK: You saw for yourself.

ULFHEJM: And the strange lady, too?

RUBEK: Yes, as you see. *(With a glance at Maja.)* The strange lady and I plan never to go on separate paths from now on.

ULFHEJM: Didn't you know the path you took is a deadly one?

RUBEK: We two tried it, just the same. Because it didn't seem too bad at first.

ULFHEJM: No, nothing seems too bad at first. But then you come to a tight corner where there's no going forward or back. And there one is stuck fast, Professor! Rock-trapped, we hunters call it.

RUBEK: *(Smiling as he looks at him.)* Are these meant for words of wisdom, Mr. Ulfhejm?

ULFHEJM: The lord forbid I should go in for words of wisdom. *(Urgently, pointing up to the peaks.)* But don't you see there's a storm gathering over our heads? Can't you hear the gusts of wind?

RUBEK: *(Listening.)* It sounds like the overture to Resurrection Day.

ULFHEJM: They're the storm blasts from the peaks, man! See how the clouds are convulsed, rolling and sinking. They'll soon be wrapping around us like a winding sheet.

IRENE: *(Starting.)* I know that winding sheet.

MAJA: *(Tugging at him.)* Let's see about getting down.

ULFHEJM: *(To Rubek.)* I can't help more than one. Stay in the hut so long as — until the storm's over. I'll send people to fetch you both —

IRENE: *(Crying out.)* Fetch us! No! No! —

ULFHEJM: *(Harshly.)* To take you by force, if necessary. It's now become a matter of life and death here. Now you know. *(To Maja.)* Come then — and put your trust in your partner's strength.

MAJA: *(Clinging to him.)* God, if I manage to get down in my whole skin, I shall sing and dance for joy.

ULFHEJM: *(Begins the climb down and calls to the others.)* Make sure you wait there in the hut till the men come with ropes to fetch you.

(Ulfhejm, with Maja in his arms, clambers quickly but carefully down into the chasm.)

IRENE: *(Looking awhile with terrified eyes at Rubek.)* Did you hear that, Arnold? Men are going to come and fetch me! Many men will come here —

RUBEK: Just keep calm, Irene.

IRENE: *(In mounting fear.)* And she — the one in black — she'll be with them. For she must have missed me long ago. And then she will seize hold of me, Arnold! And put me in the straightjacket. Yes, because she keeps one with her in her box. I've seen it myself —

RUBEK: No one will be allowed to harm you.

IRENE: *(With a manic smile.)* Ah, no, I've my own remedy for that.

RUBEK: What remedy do you mean?

IRENE: *(Drawing out the knife.)* This!

RUBEK: *(Grabbing for the knife.)* You've a knife!

IRENE: Always, always. Both day and night. In bed, too.

RUBEK: Give me the knife, Irene!

IRENE: *(Hiding it.)* You're not having it. I may well find a use for it.

RUBEK: What would you want to use it for here?

IRENE: *(Looking fixedly at him.)* It was meant for you, Arnold.

RUBEK: For *me!*

IRENE: When we sat by Lake Taunitz last night.

RUBEK: By Lake Taunitz — ?

IRENE: In front of the farmhouse. And we played with swans and waterlilies —

RUBEK: And then? And then?

IRENE: And I heard you say, in a voice as cold as ice, out of the grave, that I was nothing more than an episode in your life —

RUBEK: It was you who said that, Irene! Not I.

IRENE: *(Continuing.)* I had the knife out already. I wanted to plunge it into your back.

RUBEK: *(Darkly.)* Then why didn't you?

IRENE: Because it became horribly apparent to me you were already dead — had been dead a long time.

RUBEK: Dead?

IRENE: Dead. Dead. You as well as I. There we sat, by Lake Taunitz, we two clammy corpses, playing games with each other.

RUBEK: I don't call that dead. But you don't understand me.

IRENE: Where is that burning desire for me that you strove and fought against when I stood freely before you as the woman risen from the dead?

RUBEK: Our love is not dead, Irene.

IRENE: That love belongs to the life of earth — that beautiful, miraculous earthlife, so full of mysteries — *that* is dead in both of us.

RUBEK: *(Ardently.)* I tell you, that same love seethes and burns in me now as fiercely as ever it did before.

IRENE: And I? Have you forgotten what I am now?

RUBEK: You can choose to be whoever and whatever you want with me. For me, you're the woman I dream of you being.

IRENE: I've stood on the stage — naked — and showed myself before hundreds of men — after you.

RUBEK: It was I who drove you onto that stage — blind as I was at the time! I set that dead image of clay above the joy of life and love.

IRENE: *(Eyes downcast.)* Too late. Too late.

RUBEK: Everything that lies between then and now has not lowered you a hair's breadth in my eyes.

IRENE: *(Her head raised.)* Nor in mine, either.

RUBEK: Well then! So we are free. And there's still time for us to live our lives, Irene!

IRENE: *(Regarding him sadly.)* The desire for life died in me, Arnold. Now I am risen. And I search for you and find you. And then discover that both you and life lie dead — just as I lay dead.

RUBEK: Oh, you are deluded! Life within us and around us still seethes and surges as it ever did!

IRENE: *(Smiling and shaking her head.)* Your young woman risen from the dead sees the whole of life as laid out in a morgue.

RUBEK: *(Throws his arms ardently around her.)* Then let us two dead souls live life to the full for once — before we go down into our graves again!

IRENE: *(With a cry.)* Arnold!

RUBEK: But not here in this half light. Not here with this hideous, wet grave cloth flapping about us —

IRENE: *(In mounting passion.)* No, no — up into the light glittering in all its glory. Up to the promised mountain peaks.

RUBEK: And up there we'll celebrate our marriage feast, Irene — my beloved.

IRENE: *(Proudly.)* The sun will look gladly on us, Arnold.

RUBEK: All the powers of light may look gladly on us. And those of darkness, too. *(Grasping her hands.)* Will you now follow me, my bride, redeemed and blest?

IRENE: *(As if transfigured.)* Gladly and willingly, I follow my lord and master.

RUBEK: *(Leading her.)* First we must go through the mist, Irene, and then —

IRENE: Yes, through all the mists. And then right up to the top of the tower that gleams in the sunrise.

(The clouds of mist close densely over the landscape. Rubek and Irene, hand in hand, climb up over the snowfield to the right and soon disappear into the lower clouds. Sharp gusts of wind swirl and whine through the air. The Nun comes up over the rock slope to the left. She remains standing there, peering about silently.)

MAJA: *(Can be heard joyfully singing from far below.)*
I am free! I am free! I am free!
No more life in a mancage for me!
I am free as a bird! I am free!

(Suddenly, a sound like a thunderous roar is heard from above the snow-field. It rushes down, whirling at a terrifying speed. Rubek and Irene are obscurely glimpsed, whirled in the mass of snow and buried in it.)

THE NUN: *(Lets out a shriek, reaches out her arms toward them, and cries.)*
Irene! *(She stands silently awhile, makes the sign of the cross in the air in front of her, and says.)* Pax vobiscum!

(Maja's rejoicing and song continue from farther down the mountain.)

****

Ibsen

THE READING ROOM

YOUNG ACTORS AND THEIR TEACHERS

Haugen, Einar. *Ibsen's Drama: Author to Audience*. Minneapolis: University of Minnesota Press, 1979.

Knight, G. Wilson. *Henrik Ibsen*. New York: Grove Press, 1963.

McFarlane, James. *The Cambridge Companion to Ibsen*. Cambridge: Cambridge University Press, 1994.

Marker, Frederick J., and Lise-Lone Marker. *Ibsen's Lively Art: A Performance Study of the Major Plays*. Cambridge: Cambridge University Press, 1989.

Robins, Elizabeth. *Ibsen and the Actress*. London: Leonard & Virginia Woolf, 1928.

SCHOLARS, STUDENTS, PROFESSORS

Archer, William. *From Ibsen's Workshop: The Genesis of His Dramas*. New York: Scribner, 1911.

_____. *The Old Drama and the New*. London: Heinemann, 1923.

Bentley, Eric. *The Playwright as Thinker*. rev. ed. San Diego: Harcourt Brace Jovanovich, 1987.

Binding, Paul. *With Vine-Leaves in His Hair: The Role of the Artist in Ibsen's Plays*. Norwich, UK: Norvik Press, 2006.

Bloom, Harold, ed. *Henrik Ibsen*. Broomall, Pa.: Chelsea House Publishers, 2000

Brandes, Georg. *Henrik Ibsen: A Critical Study,* with a forty-two-page essay on Bjørnsterne Bjørnson. New York: B. Blom, 1964.

Downs, Brian W. *Ibsen: The Intellectual Background*. Cambridge: Cambridge University Press, 1948.

This extensive bibliography lists books about the playwright according to whom the books might be of interest. If you would like to research further something that interests you in the text, lists of references, sources cited, and editions used in this book are found in this section.

Durbach, Errol. *"Ibsen the Romantic": Analogues of Paradise in the Later Plays*. Athens: University of Georgia Press, 1981.

_____, ed. *Ibsen and the Theatre: Essays in Celebration of the 150th Anniversary of Henrik Ibsen's Birth*. London: Macmillan, 1980.

Ferguson, Robert. *Henrik Ibsen: A New Biography*. London: Richard Cohen Books, 1996.

Goldman, Emma. *The Social Significance of the Modern Drama*. Boston: R. G. Badger, 1914.

Gosse, Edmund. *Ibsen*. London: Hodder and Stoughton, 1907.

Grene, David. *Reality and the Heroic Pattern: Last Plays of Ibsen, Shakespeare, and Sophocles*. Chicago: University of Chicago Press, 1967.

-Holtan, Orley I. *Mythic Patterns in Ibsen's Last Plays*. Minneapolis: University of Minnesota Press, 1970.

Hornby, Richard. *Patterns in Ibsen's Middle Plays*. Lewisburg, Pa.: Bucknell University Press, 1981.

Jacobsen, Per Schelde, and Barbara Fass Leavy. *Ibsen's Forsaken Merman: Folklore in the Late Plays*. New York: New York University Press, 1988.

Johnston, Brian. *The Ibsen Cycle: The Design of the Plays from Pillars of Society to When We Dead Awaken*. rev. ed. University Park: Pennsylvania State University Press, 1992 (first published 1975).

_____. *To the Third Empire: Ibsen's Early Drama*. Minneapolis: University of Minnesota Press, 1980.

Koht, Halvdan. *The Life of Ibsen*. London: George Allen & Unwin Ltd., 1931.

Lebowitz, Naomi. *Ibsen and the Great World*. Baton Rouge: Louisiana State University Press, 1990.

Lee, Jennette. *The Ibsen Secret: A Key to the Prose Dramas of Henrik Ibsen*. Honolulu: University Press of the Pacific, 2001 (first published 1907).

McFarlane, James. *Ibsen and Meaning: Studies, Essays, and Prefaces 1953–87*. Norwich, UK: Norvik Press, 1989.

Moi, Toril. *Henrik Ibsen and the Birth of Modernism: Art, Theater, Philosophy*. Oxford: Oxford University Press, 2006.

Northam, John. *Ibsen's Dramatic Method*. London: Faber and Faber, 1953.

_____. *Ibsen: A Critical Study*. Cambridge: Cambridge University Press, 1973.

Shafer, Yvonne. *Henrik Ibsen: Life, Work, and Criticism*. Fredericton, N.B., Canada: York Press, 1985.

Shaw, Bernard. *The Quintessence of Ibsenism; Now Completed to the Death of Ibsen*. London: Constable and Co., 1922 (Dover reprint, 1994).

Templeton, Joan. *Ibsen's Women*. Cambridge: Cambridge University Press, 1997.

Tennant, P. F. D. *Ibsen's Dramatic Technique*. New York: Humanities Press, 1965.

Weigand, Hermann J. *The Modern Ibsen: A Reconsideration*. New York: Dutton, 1960.

THEATERS, PRODUCERS

Fjelde, Rolf, ed. *Ibsen: A Collection of Critical Essays*. Englewood Cliffs, N.J.: Prentice-Hall, 1965.

Gilman, Richard. *The Making of Modern Drama*. New York: Farrar, Straus and Giroux, 1974.

Lyons, Charles R., ed. *Critical Essays on Henrik Ibsen*. Boston: G. K. Hall, 1987.

Robinson, Michael, ed. *Turning the Century: Centennial Essays on Ibsen*. Norwich, UK: Norvik Press, 2007.

Schanke, Robert A. *Ibsen in America: A Century of Change*. Metuchen, N.J.: Scarecrow Press, 1988.

Valency, Maurice. *The Flower and the Castle, An Introduction to Modern Drama*. New York: Macmillan, 1963.

ACTORS, DIRECTORS, PROFESSIONALS

Andreas-Salomé, Lou. *Ibsen's Heroines*. Edited, translated and with an introduction by Siegfried Mandel. New York: Limelight Editions, 1989 (first published 1910).

Bradbrook, M. C. *Ibsen the Norwegian: A Revaluation*. London: Chatto & Windus, 1966.

Brustein, Robert. *The Theatre of Revolt: An Approach to Modern Drama*. Chicago: Ivan R. Dee, 1991 (first published 1964).

Davis, Rick, and Brian Johnston, trans. *Ibsen: Four Major Plays*. Hanover, N.H.: Smith and Kraus Publishers, Inc., 1994.

_____, trans. *Ibsen: Volume II, Four Plays*. Hanover, N.H.: Smith and Kraus Publishers, Inc., 1996.

_____, trans. *Ibsen: Volume III, Four Plays*. Hanover, N.H.: Smith and Kraus Publishers, Inc., 1998.

Fergusson, Francis. *The Idea of a Theater, a Study of Ten Plays: The Art of Drama in Changing Perspective*. Princeton, N.J.: Princeton University Press, 1949.

Goldman, Michael. *Ibsen: The Dramaturgy of Fear*. New York: Columbia University Press, 1999.

Johnston, Brian, trans. *Text and Supertext in Ibsen's Drama*. University Park: Pennsylvania State University Press, 1989.

_____. *Emperor and Galilean*. Hanover, N.H.: Smith and Kraus Publishers, Inc., 1999.

_____, ed. *Ibsen's Selected Plays* (A Norton Critical Edition). New York: W. W. Norton & Co., 2004.

Marinelli, Donald, ed. *Henrik Ibsen's Ghosts: A Dramaturgical Sourcebook*. With Rick Davis and Brian Johnston. Pittsburgh: Carnegie Mellon University Press, 1997.

THE EDITIONS OF IBSEN'S WORKS USED FOR THIS BOOK

Davis, Rick, and Brian Johnston, trans. *Ibsen: Four Major Plays*. Hanover, N.H.: Smith and Kraus, 1994.

Johnston, Brian, with Rick Davis, trans. *Ibsen: Volume III: Four Plays*. Hanover, N.H.: Smith and Kraus, 1998.

Johnston, Brian, ed. *Ibsen's Selected Plays* (A Norton Critical Edition). New York: W. W. Norton & Co., 2004.

SOURCES CITED IN THIS BOOK

Archer, William, in Michael Meyer, *Ibsen*. London: Rupert Hart-Davis, 1971, p. 659.

Casanova, Pascal. *The World Republic of Letters*. Cambridge: Harvard University Press, 2005, p. 162.

Ibsen, Henrik. *Letters and Speeches*. Evert Sprinchorn, ed. New York: Hill and Wang, 1964, p. 337.

James, Henry. *Essays in London and Elsewhere*. London: J. R. Osgood, McIlvaine and Co., 1893.

_____. *The Scenic Art: Notes on Acting and the Drama, 1972–1901*. Allan Wade, ed. New Brunswick, N.J.: Rutgers University Press, 1948.

Joyce, James. *The Critical Writings of James Joyce.* Ellsworth Mason and Richard Ellmann, eds. New York: Viking Press, 1964.

Meyer, Michael. *Henrik Ibsen* (3 vol. biography). London: Rupert Hart-Davis, 1971.

Shaw, George Bernard. *Dramatic Opinions and Essays.* New York: Brentano's, 1928.

INDEX

The entries in the index include highlights from the main In an Hour essay portion of the book.

84

ABOUT THE AUTHORS

Rick Davis, Associate Provost for Undergraduate Education at George Mason University, also serves as Professor of Theater and Co-Artistic Director of Theater of the First Amendment (TFA). Under his leadership, TFA, Mason's resident Equity theater, has been nominated for thirty-eight Helen Hayes Awards and has won the award twelve times, including outstanding resident production and outstanding new play.

Prior to coming to Mason in 1991, Rick worked for six seasons at Baltimore's Center Stage, as Resident Dramaturg and Associate Artistic Director, and co-founded Pittsburgh's American Ibsen Theater. A member of the Society of Stage Directors and Choreographers, he has directed theater and opera in professional venues across the country as well as dozens of college and university productions. He has served as a National Endowment for the Arts panelist on many occasions, and as a site visitor for more than twenty years.

Rick's volume of translations and commentaries, *Calderón de la Barca: Four Great Plays of the Golden Age*, was published by Smith and Kraus in 2009. He is also the co-author of three books, *Ibsen: Four Major Plays* (1994) and *Ibsen in an Hour* with Brian Johnston, and *Writing About Theatre* (1999) with Christopher Thaiss. He wrote the libretto for *Love's Comedy*, an opera by composer Kim D. Sherman. He and Ms. Sherman also wrote "The Songbird and the Eagle," a concert oratorio, premiered to critical acclaim in December 2006 by the San Jose Chamber Orchestra. His co-translations of Ibsen have been performed at many leading regional theaters and at many colleges and universities. He has contributed to publications such as *American Theatre, Theater, The Journal of Social History,* and *Theater Three*, and is the author of three entries in the *Columbia Encyclopedia of Modern Drama* and a major article in the new *Oxford Encyclopedia of the Modern World*.

Rick has also taught at Washington College in Chestertown, Maryland, and guest lectured at institutions such as N.Y.U., Carnegie Mellon, and Yale School of Drama. He has been a speaker or panelist at conferences such as the American Society for Theatre Research, International Federation for Theatre Research, Association for Theatre in Higher Education, Literary Managers and Dramaturgs of the Americas, Ibsen Society of America, National Ibsen Symposium, and the East-Central Theatre Conference.

At Mason he teaches directing, dramatic literature, and theater history, and he directs both theater and opera. He serves as host and Associate Producer for *Studio A*, televised conversations with notable filmmakers for GMU TV. In 1997 he was honored with Mason's Teaching Excellence Award and was named the Alumni Association "Distinguished Faculty Member of the Year" in 2006. Rick was educated at Lawrence University (B.A.) and the Yale School of Drama (M.F.A., D.F.A.).

Brian Johnston has taught at Cambridge University, England; Northwestern University, Illinois; the University of California (Berkeley and Santa Barbara); Yarmouk University and University of Amman in the Hashemite Kingdom of Jordan; from 1982 to 1986 at Beirut University College; and at the American University of Beirut, Lebanon. He joined the faculty of the School of Drama, Carnegie Mellon University, in 1986 and currently is retired (emeritus).

He published three critical studies of Ibsen: *To The Third Empire* (1980), *Text and Supertext in Ibsen's Drama* (1988), and a revised edition of *The Ibsen Cycle* (1992). Performances of his translations (with Rick Davis) of Ibsen include *A Doll House* (Center Stage, Baltimore), *An Enemy of the People* (Center Stage, Baltimore and Perseverance Theater, Alaska), *Hedda Gabler* and *The Lady from the Sea* (George Mason University), *Rosmersholm* (Washington Shakespeare Company, D.C.); and *Little Eyolf* (University of Toledo, Ohio).

Brian edited the journal *Theater Three* between 1986 and 1991. He has lectured on Ibsen extensively in the United States and internationally. Four volumes of his translations have been published by Smith and Kraus: *Ibsen: Four Major Plays*, translated by Rick Davis and Brian Johnston, 1994; *Ibsen: Volume II Four Plays*, 1996, by Brian Johnston; and, with Rick Davis, *Ibsen: Volume III: Four Plays*, 1998. His translation of *Emperor and Galilean* was published in 1999. He edited the Norton Critical Edition of *Ibsen's Selected Plays*, published in 2004. It includes his new translation of *Peer Gynt*. In 2009 Smith and Kraus will publish an electronic edition of *Love's Comedy* (currently online as a PDF file on Brian Johnston's Web site at: www.ibsenvoyages.com).

ACKNOWLEDGMENTS

Special thanks to Jim Maiwurm for research assistance.

Smith and Kraus, Inc. wishes to thank Rick Davis and Brian Johnston, whose enlightened permissions policies reflect an understanding that copyright law is intended to both protect the rights of creators of intellectual property as well as to encourage its use for the public good.

Know the playwright,
love the play.

Open a new door to theater study, performance, and audience satisfaction with these Playwrights In an Hour titles.

ANCIENT GREEK

Aeschylus   Aristophanes   Euripides   Sophocles

RENAISSANCE

William Shakespeare

MODERN

Anton Chekhov   Noël Coward   Lorraine Hansberry
Henrik Ibsen   Arthur Miller   Molière   Eugene O'Neill
Arthur Schnitzler   George Bernard Shaw   August Strindberg
Frank Wedekind   Oscar Wilde   Thornton Wilder
Tennessee Williams

CONTEMPORARY

Edward Albee   Alan Ayckbourn   Samuel Beckett
Theresa Rebeck   Sarah Ruhl   Sam Shepard   Tom Stoppard
August Wilson

To purchase or for more information
visit our web site inanhourbooks.com